The Father's Love Language
Discovering the Depth of Yahweh Hidden in the Hebrew Language

Angie Sickler

3 TREES

The Father's Love Language Discovering the Depth of Yahweh Hidden in the Hebrew Language

Copyright ©2024 by Angie Sickler

All rights reserved.

3 Trees Publishing 18024 Dedeaux Clan Road Gulfport MS 39503

3Treespublishing@gmail.com

ISBN: 979-8-9864862-3-9 print

ISBN: 979-8-9864862-4-6 ebook

LCCN: 2024910449

Cover Design: Roseanne Sather zansather@gmail.com

Contents

Foreword

To be honest, I struggled with whether to write this book or not. In the world's eyes I'm just a midwestern homemaker with a healthy love of all things sci-fi, but I know that's not all God sees. So, in writing this book, I'm operating on the value He sees in me – a value he recently reminded me. You see, I've been considering writing this type of book for awhile now, but just wasn't sure....and then a ministry friend of mine, Rachel Lish, texted me out of the blue with a simple suggestion – "You should write a book on how to study all this Hebrew stuff!" And then my mentor, Papa Anthony Turner, told our mentorship group that we need to come up with 3 goals for our respective ministries. This book is one of mine. God is so good – taking something that was already on my mind and putting it on someone else's mind to push me in the right direction. I am so blessed to be called His and so blessed to have friends who listen to Him, too.

I also need to give a shout out to my amazing support and biggest fan - my husband George. He has not only supported our family financially and spiritually since 1999, but he was the first to suggest that I start making my journal entries into teaching videos and a traveling ministry. Both literally and figuratively, I could never have done any of this without him.

So, if you've purchased or have been gifted with this book, I hope it blesses you as much as learning all of this has blessed me in ways that I'll make plain in the next several pages. If you gain nothing else from this book, my prayer is that in seeing God's word through the lens of his love language and feasts prescribed for his people, the Holy Spirit will cause the Word of God to open up to you in ways you never imagined. This is an amazing time to be alive and the Holy Spirit is eager to speak to us about the past, present, and future through His Word. Let's get started!

Bereshit - In the Beginning
בראשית

"In the beginning...." Genesis 1:1a

It was late 2019 and I had just finished a hard day of home repairs in anticipation of putting our house on the market. My husband asked me "Have you ever heard of the Bereshit prophecy? You have to see this guy...". And with that first video of John Kostik explaining the Bereshit prophecy, I was hooked!

Before we dive into that fascinating word in the Bible, let me briefly tell you about where I was in life at this time. I started following Jesus at the age of 19 after a terrible year of domestic abuse and crime (that's a story for another day). After that I was briefly married, became a mother, and then my husband left me...all by the age of 21. I remarried in 1999 at the age of 23 to my current husband, George. Together we raised our combined family of 5 kids - 4 of whom are now adults, with the 5th still a teen at home with us. In our church involvement we've always held some place in ministry – at times volunteering and at times being paid staff. In fact, we've been blessed with the opportunity to serve in every aspect of church ministry except for head pastor. We did our best to balance family, work, and ministry. Our adult kids are all married and the 3 oldest have kids of their own, which means we have become grandparents! With all of our kids moving on with life, we were faced with a large house we no longer needed, and the housing market was great for sellers, so we started fixing up the place to sell. Everything looked great for us from a worldly perspective.... but spiritually I was feeling blah.

We've all had those periods of blah in our spiritual walk, haven't we? Days, weeks, or months where we feel like we're just going through the motions – go to church once or twice a week, then every morning get up, pray briefly, read the bible for 15 min, if that, and move on with the day. I knew I had to do something different to reignite my passion in my relationship with Christ. I just didn't know how. And then I started following a great guy online: John Kostik.

We'll start with the content from his video on the Bereshit prophecy because that's where I started in my fascination and treasure hunting using God's love language – Hebrew!

Bereshit is the first word of the bible. It's a Hebrew word that means "In the beginning".

The Hebrew word "Bereshit" looks like this: בראשית

We read Hebrew from right to left, so it is spelled bet-resh-aleph-shin-yod-tav.

Bet-resh is the Hebrew word "Bar" which means son.

Bet-resh-aleph is the Hebrew word "Bara" which means creator.

Shin means destroy.

Yod means hand.

Tav is the cross which also means covenant.

So in the first word of the Bible, God spells out his plan: The son, our creator, will be destroyed by his own hand on a cross, for the sake of a covenant.

Can you see, with just one word, how exciting this is? The next thought that occurred to me was "I wonder what other hidden treasures can be found in God's Word in this way!" God was birthing a new way of thinking in me and I didn't even know it quite yet.

With that curious thought I found a few resources to help me and I began looking at all kinds of words: praise and worship words, the names in Jesus' lineage, fruits of the spirit, the seven spirits of the Lord, Psalm 119, on and on and on. I couldn't get enough. In fact, we now joke that throughout that first year there were numerous times when George reminded me that maybe I should get out of my pajamas, brush my teeth, eat something, etc. I found myself so engrossed in worship and study that I didn't want to peel myself away even for a moment! I had fallen in love with Jesus all over again.

The more I opened up scripture to look into Hebrew concepts, the more I realized just how many places God has placed his message in his chosen people's language. In this book we'll look at just 3 such places: The Word of God, God's Appointed Times, and The Night Sky. I truly hope you'll find a new "bereshit" – a new beginning – in your time with the Lord and in your good news invitation to a lost and dying world.

. . .

So how did my new beginning unfold? Well, I'm not a scholar, nor a rabbi. I don't even have a college degree. I'm not Jewish by physical lineage, nor have I ever joined the religion of Judaism. I'm simply a child of God who is beginning to recognize her true nature within God's grand plan – which starts with our identity in Christ.

Nokhri, Ger, Ben - Foreigner, Stranger, Son – נֵכָר גֵּר בֵּן

"And the LORD said to Moses and Aaron, "This is the ordinance of the Passover: No foreigner shall eat it." Exodus 12:43

"'The stranger who dwells among you shall be to you as one born among you, and you shall love him as yourself." Leviticus 19:34a

For you did not receive the spirit of bondage again to fear, but you received the Spirit of adoption by whom we cry out, "Abba, Father." Romans 8:15

In ancient Israel there were 3 classifications of people: nokhri (foreigner), ger (stranger), and ben (son). If you were a foreigner, you had some rights but not equal with a son of Israel – there were certain things you could not participate in but the law would still treat you with decency. If you were a stranger, that meant that, though you were previously just a foreigner living in the land, you'd have stated your intent to become a Hebrew person and had done all necessary rites of passage in order to do so – you had equal rights and could participate in all of the Hebrew customs and proceedings, but you had no inheritance. If you were a son, you had all available national and spiritual rights AND an inheritance. These levels set you apart from the others. Adoption did happen but it was obligatory by family – by law the nearest blood relative had to take in any orphaned relatives. There is really no ancient Hebrew word in the Bible for adoption but there is a phrase used in the story of Moses that the pharaoh's daughter took him and he "haya ben" or "became a son".

However, upon the beginning of our new covenant with Christ, Paul writes that we have been adopted! That term "yhiothesia" or "adoption" in Greek is a new concept because it involves choice, not obligation. Within Roman society, it was common for a rich man to choose to adopt a child or even an adult who seems like he'd be a good fit for his family. By rights that newly adopted son or daughter would gain all of that father's inheritance – even in life! All that the father owns, the child now owns. All decision-making regarding land, servants, and wealth is now just as much on the son as it is on the father. The father has given equal ownership of all he has. Adoption means you not only have equal rights but you ALSO have an inheritance!

So, that's a nice history lesson and all, but what does that have to do with us? How does being adopted into the family of God include all things Hebrew?

Before I answer that question, I will put a huge disclaimer here... whether or not you choose to become Hebrew minded, if Jesus is your Lord and Savior you are saved by faith in Christ. The Hebrew celebrations, months, language, etc. are for your benefit - they carry blessings for the children of God! So, whether you decide to participate or not, just know that if you believe that Jesus is the Messiah who died for your sins and rose again and you confess Him as Lord, you are a beloved and valuable member of the body of Christ. The only question you now must ask is – do you want more of Him?

Now, to get back to that first question, let's look at those 3 categories in the ways they exist still today. We still have foreigners, strangers, and sons within our church meetings. A foreigner is anyone who is not a believer, but they pop in and out of churches whenever a holiday comes around or they face difficulty in life and need some compassion. Not only do they not experience the benefits of fellowship with believers, but they also have no salvation – no inheritance. A stranger amongst us is someone who is very involved in church culture. They do all of the church things – they're always helping out with church functions, volunteering as a greeter every Sunday, and doing everything they know to do in order to fit into church culture, but they aren't believers. They treat church like a social club, so they'll have all kinds of favor with people in church circles but won't have an inheritance. Our hope for both foreigners and strangers is that they will one day drop the façade and fall on their knees in true repentance and acceptance of salvation. Now, if you have been saved by faith, you're not a foreigner or a stranger. You are an adopted son or daughter with an inheritance. But your mindset will determine whether or not you've fully committed to your adoption - fully reaping all of the benefits of being a son.

According to biblical scholar and author Robert Heidler there are 3 different mindsets known to all men since the days of Christ on earth: Barbaric thinking, Greek thinking, Hebraic thinking. Barbaric tribal thinking is dominated by fear. Everything is about survival - defense and offense in every area of life. Greek thinking is dominated by intellect. If it can't be explained rationally, it's not important. Hebraic thinking is dominated by God. If God says it, then it's true and I will apply that to my everyday life.

. . .

Many American Christians have struggled to understand the Hebraic mind of God using our Greek or Barbaric thinking. It's why we now have several church groups completely abandoning the Old Testament either purposefully or passively - because some of the grander stories in the Old Testament don't make sense or have no relevancy to a Greek mind. It's why some Christians are just fine with supporting abortion...a Barbaric thinker doesn't understand why that would be wrong, because abortion is about their own "survival" or some poor teen girl's "survival". They can't think outside of survival. We need to get to a place where we accept the truth of God's Word as true no matter what we feel. We need to change our mindset through fully committing to every aspect of our adoption.

So let's revisit some verses we've read before and really think through them with this new Hebraic lens.

"Understand, then, that those who have faith are children of Abraham."
    Galatians 3:7

Does this mean we have to follow Torah laws? No...Jesus summed up all the law into just 2 laws:

    1. Love the lord your God with all your heart soul, mind, and strength.
    2. Love your neighbor as yourself.

Did he offer the same summation for Hebrew celebrations, or language? Nope! It was the Greek thinking Roman Catholic church that rejected Hebrew feasts, created their own holidays to celebrate saints instead of God, and insisted on continuing their idolatry-born calendar rather than adopting God's calendar. And then it was that same weak church that placated the barbarians to barter for their salvation by mixing saintly celebrations with barbaric holidays. keeping us all in Greek and Barbaric thinking for centuries!

Just to give you an example of this, let's look at part of a letter written by a member of the Council of Nicea on May 20, 325 AD:

" We also send you the good news of the settlement concerning the holy Pasch, namely that in answer to your prayers this question also has been resolved. All the brethren in the East who have hitherto followed the Jewish practice will henceforth observe the custom of the Romans and of yourselves and of all of us who from ancient times have kept Easter together with you."

While the Council of Nicea bore good fruit, it also was the beginning of the end of our Hebrew roots as Christians. Slowly many in the Church have begun to realize the importance of these roots.

So why choose to celebrate Hebrew holidays, culture, and language? A few reasons:

The most important reason is that I want to have the mind of Christ. Not only did he live a very Hebrew way of life, but he also CREATED that way of life and gave it to his chosen people. If I want to have his mind, I need to seek to think like he thinks in every aspect.

. . .

I also think that an adopted child should embrace every aspect of his adoptive family. Think about it: the Israelite's language, laws, and customs were ordained by God for his people, and we have been grafted in...adopted. When a child is adopted into a new family, does that child continue to follow the traditions and celebrations from his old life or does he celebrate new traditions with his new family? And if you, as an adopted child, chose to only celebrate your old traditions, you'd be missing out on family fun and gifts, right?! I don't want to miss out anymore. I want to fully embrace my adopted family!

Another reason – I do it for the blessings! There are so many promised blessings for those who obey God's commands (which includes the Lord's feasts). A short list is found in Deuteronomy 28: prominence over other nations, success in whatever you do, prosperity in children, food, and livestock, power over enemies for protection, bountiful harvests, blessings on the work of your hands so that you might be the giver, not the borrower, you will be the head and not the tail. Furthermore Proverbs 3:9,10 gives the specific example of blessings for those who celebrate First Fruits: "Honor the Lord with your wealth, with the firstfruits of all your crops; then your barns will be filled to overflowing, and your vats will brim over with new wine."

Also, I want to make the Israelites of today JEALOUS!! You don't think that's an appropriate goal? Let's read...

"I am saying all this especially for you Gentiles. God has appointed me as the apostle to the Gentiles. I stress this, for **I want somehow to make the people of Israel jealous** of what you Gentiles have, so I might save some of them. For since their rejection meant that God offered salvation to the rest of the world, their acceptance will be even more wonderful. It will be life for those who were dead!

If the part of the dough offered as firstfruits is holy, then the whole batch is holy. For if the roots of the tree are holy, the branches will be, too. But some of these branches from Abraham's tree—some of the people of Israel—have been broken off. And you Gentiles, who were branches from a wild olive tree, have been grafted in. So now you also receive the blessing God has promised Abraham and his children, sharing in the rich nourishment from the root of God's special olive tree. But you must not brag about being grafted in to replace the branches that were broken off. You are just a branch, not the root."

Romans 11:13-18

Notice three things in that passage: jealousy, a root, and firstfruits.

Our relationship with God should make the Israelites jealous so that they will want to join in and not be left out. That's a good goal....how exactly will we make them jealous unless we are celebrating THEIR feasts and worshipping THEIR God just as they do or better with more passion than they do? Jewish people today, while generally respectful of our faith in Jesus, are not jealous at all. Why would they be? They think we worship a false Messiah and a false God because they don't see us following any of the things God prescribed for his people. Let's show them how to worship God with passion during his feasts and celebrations! Let's show them how we dig into God's Word in the original written language! In showing that we understand our adoption and follow God's prescribed feasts just like they do, only then will we stir up that jealousy within them!

Also – we are branches grafted in but we are not the root. Who is the root? Throughout the bible 3 important roots are mentioned: the root of Jesse and the root of David are one and the same – Jesus. The other root, however, is the root of Jacob which is the nation of Israel. Whether this verse in Romans is referring to Jesus or the entire nation of Israel is irrelevant...because they both followed Hebrew customs, feasts, and torah. So if Jesus and Israel (or rather God's Israel – the way he shaped it) are the root and we are the branches, we should feed off the root and grow from it. And if we want more growth, we must feed off the WHOLE root...not just the non-Hebrew parts of it. Our root is Hebrew....so I am fed by that Hebrew nature.

The principle of a firstfruits offering mentioned in that verse is present not only in the actual Spring Feast of Firstfruits, but also at every Rosh Chodesh (head of the month). At the time of the writing of this book, George and I lead a monthly worship service and teaching for every new Hebrew month as we look into what God has done historically and thematically throughout his Word.

While studying the fourth month, I found this passage where in the fourth month Zechariah heard this from God regarding events in the end times:

""This is what the Lord of Heaven's Armies says: People from nations and cities around the world will travel to Jerusalem. The people of one city will say to the people of another, 'Come with us to Jerusalem to ask the Lord to bless us. Let's worship the Lord of Heaven's Armies. I'm determined to go.' Many peoples and powerful nations will come to Jerusalem to seek the Lord of Heaven's Armies and to ask for his blessing. "This is what the Lord of Heaven's Armies says: In those days ten men from different nations and languages of the world will clutch at the sleeve of one Jew. And they will say, 'Please let us walk with you, for we have heard that God is with you.'""

Zechariah 8:20-23

. . .

It's me. It's you. We're the ones now leaning towards a Hebrew mindset. We're the ones seeking to "walk with the Jews" - in other words we want to learn to walk and talk as they did because unlike the barbarian or Greek thinking we've grown up in, Hebrew thinking (including the language) was ordained and directed by God for his people. And I believe by us diving into the Hebrew mindset in our worship and celebrations that it will cause a jealous longing in the people of Israel which will prompt curiosity, which will turn into salvation. Let's be praying for that as we seek to live as if we are TRULY adopted sons and daughters of the God of Israel!

The Father's Love Language In:

The Word of God

Musar - Instruction - מוּסָר

"Take firm hold of instruction, do not let go; Keep her, for she is your life." Proverbs 4:13

In this chapter I'd like to show you the way in which the Lord has shown me how to enter into an intimate time with him and then dig into the Word and the Hebrew letters to reveal mysteries that God wants to show to you. If, after reading this chapter, you decide that though this looks like an interesting and fun way to study God's Word, it's just not for you – great! All that means is that you get to discover your own interesting and fun way to study God's Word. Whatever method of praise, prayer and study you use, the most important thing is that you do it and enjoy it!

First, I want us to start with the understanding that we are to let Jesus lead. We seem to understand the need to have Him lead in our marriages, our parenting, our work, etc. But for some reason we, including myself, have – for far too long – led our own quiet time with God. We pick the time, the worship music (if any at all), the chapter we're going to read, how our conversation in prayer goes, and the time we leave. What do you think might happen if we let Christ choose all those things for us? How much more might we get from our time with God if we let him lead in this area, too?

So, as you peruse through the next set of instructions, you'll see that phrase often: "Let Him Lead." And hopefully it will become a repeating mantra in our minds as we sit down to spend time with Him each day.

One other thing, before we jump into the step-by-step instructions, first you'll want to become familiar with the letters and numbers, and meanings of both. For reference, the back of this book contains 3 important pages:

1. The original Hebrew pictographs (so you can see how the meanings match the image)
2. The modern-day Hebrew letters with a list of meanings for each one
3. The number meanings – All numbers correspond to a Hebrew letter.

Look at these pages just to get comfortable with the letters, numbers, and meanings. Get used to reading from right to left, as well. You don't need to memorize all of it, but you will find that the more you use these tools, the more you will naturally absorb them into memory!

Before we dive into this instructional list we have to start with a solid spiritual framework. That means ripping out any old, rotted framework to make way for the new, durable one. I'm talking about what you're consuming that you shouldn't and what you're not that you should. Often when we find ourselves in a spiritual rut it's because our spiritual hunger is non-existent. It's like a person who has a New Year's resolution to start eating right. They know they should eat more meat, veggies, and fruits but they're just not hungry for those things. In order to create that hunger for good things, you first must lock away the twinkies...or throw them out. If you keep twinkies in the cupboards, every time you try to get hungry for an apple, those twinkies are staring you right in the face, begging for you to inhale them. BUT...if you throw them away or lock them up and give away the key for a time, you'll find your hunger for good food returning – because now that apple is all you have! The same applies to spiritual hunger. If you want to be hungry for the Word, consider everything else that your eyes and ears consume and choose to put them away for a time. Even if those things aren't necessarily "bad" for you, if they are filling you up so that you are no longer hungry for God's Word, then they are a dangerous distraction. If you put them away until your spiritual hunger returns, you may even be able to safely bring them out again – but only as a treat...never as the main course. God's Word is the main course, the side dish, the casserole, and the pie! If you make this temporary sacrifice to build up your hunger for the Word, you may find you're not really hungry for much else!

Once you've removed the old framework and have begun to build a new one based on your hunger for his presence, be sure to seek the Holy Spirit. The Holy Spirit is the guide. He'll show you where to build. When you meet for intimate times with the Lord (more on that in the chapter on "Yada"), remember that this is first and foremost a relationship (more on that in the chapter on "Dodi"). This is not a business transaction. So, let's cultivate our time with the Lord with that in mind.

. . .

We're going to approach the Lord on His terms, not ours. He is our father and our friend, but He is also our King. So when we come to Him for a time of intimacy we're going to enter with praise and thanksgiving. Why? Because that's how he tells us we should:

"Enter his gates with thanksgiving and his courts with praise; give thanks to him and praise his name."

Psalms 100:4

These speak of the gates and courts of the tabernacle, and where is God's tabernacle now? Inside of each of us who believe. So to open that place within us where God resides, in order to meet with him we are to enter with Toda, Tehilla, Yada, and Barak.

Toda is thanksgiving but it is also the act of holding your hands out in adoration and confession – a confession of love.

Tehilla is singing a praise song. Even if you don't like your voice, God loves to hear it!

Yada is thankfulness as you hold out your hands in reverence and knowing or acknowledging your sin and confession of that sin and a confession of your faith. But it is also the word used for "knowing" your spouse - it's intimacy!

Barak is to bless and to kneel before the king.

. . .

So, as we enter in to our time with God, we should enter correctly. Things used to be very different in my time with God. I used to sit down, read my chapter or devotional page, say a quick prayer trying to remember everything and everyone to ask God for, and then I was done. I knew I should do these things, but it often felt empty and lonely. Where was God?

Well, I was entering his presence improperly, wasn't I?

So, Psalm 100 and several other scriptures show us how to enter our time with God. We enter first with outstretched hands of adoration, singing his praise, confessing both our sin AND our love to him in reverence, knowing him intimately, and recognizing him as King. THAT is how you enter his gates to meet with him.

To that end, as he is King, we want to Let Him Lead. We're going to ask the Lord to help us choose a time of day where we don't have a time crunch (If you have little kids you might need to get up earlier, stay up later, have your spouse watch them or teach them how to do this with you.). Then we're going to Let Him Lead our praise. Ask Him "What love song would you like me to sing to you today?" and wait. If a title or tune pops into your head, find it online or on your computer and sing with it, pouring all your adoration on Him. But waiting on the Lord and hearing his voice requires practice just like anything else, so if you don't hear anything the first time, don't get discouraged. Keep trying. He IS speaking, but sometimes we need practice learning how to listen. If you've waited on the Lord for some time and nothing comes to you, still choose praise first and just pick a song. So, we're going to put on some worship music, close our eyes, and began to pour our praise and thanks on Him. "I will enter his gates with thanksgiving in my heart, I will enter his courts with

21

praise." This is how we are instructed to approach him. Even when Christ gave instruction on prayer (see The Lord's Prayer) he instructed us to start with praise and adoration, right?

After we have given Him His due praise, we're going to seek His face in the "eyes of our heart" which simply means the center of our imagination. We give that imagination to God to shape sights within it. Again, this might take practice. Keep trying! When you see Him, notice what part you see – is it his outstretched hand or his eye or his whole body? What are you two doing – laying in a field of flowers? Sitting together on a bench just gazing at each other? Walking hand in hand? In His lap, crying? Whatever it is it'll be just what you needed to see of Him in that moment. After you've spent some time with Him we are, again, going to Let Him Lead when it comes to what we see and study. We're going to ask "What do you want me to know about you right now?" If nothing comes, keep practicing! But we will wait for Him to have the first word and all we will do is wait. We will wait upon the Lord and he will often (but not always) show us a word, a phrase, a number, a letter, a bible verse, or an image. If you don't get anything specific from God, that's ok – just ask the Holy Spirit to open up his Word to you as you begin reading in any chapter of your choosing. This is treasure hunting! So, once we have something in His Word to read, we're going to look it up in scripture using these treasure hunting steps:

1. If you have a scripture in mind look it up and read it in context. If you've received just a word, phrase, or image, do an online search for anything like that in scripture. Once you find a verse that fits what you believe God was showing you, look it up and read it in context. Read your verse in a few different translations, as well. Become familiar with the verse and its surrounding verses.

2. Never dismiss curiosity. If the passage you're reading is confusing or you just feel like you're missing something in what was happening at the time or why it was happening, look it up on history websites. You might find that historic context lends a lot of understanding to the passage.

3. Look up the verse in blueletterbible.org . Once you're on the site, you'll see the search bar. Once you've looked up the verse (or the word, if the general internet search for the word gave you nothing), you'll see the whole chapter come up on the page. Find your verse and expand it by pressing the "tools" button next to the verse. That verse will expand so that you can see each English word or phrase on the left paired with its Hebrew or Greek equal on the right. In the middle column you'll see it's "Strong's number" which is usually a letter/number combination that has been assigned to that word for organization purposes. Find the word or phrase that seemed most highlighted to you and click on its Strong's number. (If you have a paper concordance, you can do the same search and study without the internet.)

4. Once you've clicked that number, a new page will open up with all the information about that word. And when I say "all", I mean "ALL"! There is so much to unpack, so don't get overwhelmed. Just peruse through all of the tools – word spelling, transliteration, pronunciation, etymology, any root word, possible meanings (there's usually quite a few for each word), all of the various English words it was translated into, outline of biblical usage, a lexicon to further explain the word and its usage, PLUS every verse in the bible in which that word is found. Learn as much about this word as you have time to.

5. Before we dive deeper into this word you have, if your word is only found in Greek there's one more step. If the word you've looked up is only found in the New Testament, the good news is usually that word in the NT will have a companion word in the OT. While inside your word page, scroll down to just before you hit the list of verses for that word. Just above the verses is the phrase "View OT results in the LXX Greek concordance". Click on it and look at the available verses for a match. If there are no OT matches in the Greek concordance, one last effort can be made by reading your NT verse in a Hebrew bible, but that's usually not necessary. If it IS necessary, however, I found a really good one online here: sarshalom.us/resources/scripture/asv/bible.html

6. Now that you have your Hebrew word and you know all you can about it, ask the Holy Spirit to show you which meanings of the letters and corresponding numbers best explains the true richness of this word. Look at each letter and jot down notes as to which meaning fits best in this word. Once you've considered all options and taken some notes, bring it all together in a cohesive sentence. If you've taken these steps, you should be able to see a deeper meaning of the word within the meanings of the letters. Once you see that deeper meaning and you've studied the definition, context, and history, you should see a lesson unfold. Write down what this means for you in your life or for Christians as a whole.

7. Thank God. Just as we started this time of intimate worship and listening to/reading God's words, so we will end the same - with a "Thank you." to the Holy Spirit for the time He spent with us and for providing guidance and revelation.

Let me give you an example of a word that I studied in this way, step by step:

One morning in worship God showed me a vision of luxurious white robes filling my sight...it seemed to go on forever, and then the words of a verse I'd read before came to me: "the train of his robe fills the temple".

1. I looked it up and read it in context. This is Isaiah 6:1 which is the beginning of a vision that Isaiah saw. In his vision God was on his throne, on a tall platform, in the temple. Angels stood above the throne and spoke praises to the Lord. Isaiah was undone in awe, and then an angel cleansed his lips with a coal from the altar and he received a message from the Lord to speak to the people of Israel.

2. A point of curiosity struck me as I wondered "Why is it important that the train of his robe fills the temple? What does that mean?", so I looked it up online. It turns out that there IS a reason that's important. In the days of Isaiah, Assyrian kings, Egyptian kings, and even previously King Solomon of Israel wore long robes while seated on a high throne so that it appeared their robes filled the throne area and the steps up to the throne. But their robes didn't start out long. They started out at the usual length, but with every victory over an enemy, the conquering king would tear off the bottom half of the enemy king's garment and sew it onto their own adding to the length. A torn and shortened robe meant shame for that enemy king. The long robe of a king showed his many victories and greatness. Isn't that amazing?! And that knowledge helps so much with the significance of this passage –

God's train fills the ENTIRE TEMPLE because he has won every victory!

3. This significance is bolstered by the information I found in looking at the word "train" in Hebrew which can mean hem, skirt, or train.

4. The Hebrew word for "train" led me to a few more words, one of which was the word for garment which showed up in Zechariah 3, where we find this story: "Then the angel showed me Jeshua the high priest standing before the angel of the Lord. The Accuser, Satan, was there at the angel's right hand, making accusations against Jeshua. And the Lord said to Satan, "I, the Lord, reject your accusations, Satan. Yes, the Lord, who has chosen Jerusalem, rebukes you. This man is like a burning stick that has been snatched from the fire." Jeshua's clothing was filthy as he stood there before the angel. So the angel said to the others standing there, "Take off his filthy clothes." And turning to Jeshua he said, "See, I have taken away your sins, and now I am giving you these fine new clothes."" He takes our filthy robes! There is also the story of how David, when he was being chased by King Saul, snuck into the cave where Saul was sleeping and tore off the corner of his robe – the word for "corner" there also means "hem" which is the bottom part of a robe. So it's likely that he tore off the bottom half of Saul's robe to claim victory and cause Saul shame without killing him. The significance of this act is also probably why David felt so bad about it afterwards.

5. This time I did not need this step.

6. The word that seemed most highlighted to me in this passage was the word for train, so I wrote it out like this:

Train (of his robe) - sul- שׁוּל
Shin-vav-lamedh

From the letters: Victories joined together and leading out.

You can see how I got these meanings (and verified them with the Holy Spirit) by looking at the Hebrew letters page: the letter shin is also the number 300 which signifies supernatural victory, the letter vav can mean joining things together (because it's a nail), and the letter lamedh means to lead (because it's a shepherd's staff).

The lessons I learned from this treasure hunt are twofold:

1. Whenever I choose to allow God to take away Satan's garments of sin and accusation that's on me, I am allowing God to add to his glory and greatness. I actually do him a GREAT SERVICE by giving up those garments to him. Then he covers me with new clean garments.
2. In this time of great uncertainty in the world we are seeing all kinds of sin being uncovered. Sometimes we look at it in despair or fear, but God is telling you that this is just him ripping off Satan's garments to expose his great shame. We should rejoice in this, for while God rips that away, he is sewing it onto his own robe, adding to his greatness and glory!

Hopefully seeing that process in action helps you see how exciting and effective this can be! I've learned so much by digging, and I hope you will, too!

So, let's take a deep dive into the language, months, and feasts from a Christian perspective.

Aleph-Bet - Alphabet - א-ב

Genesis 11:1

"Now the whole earth had one language and one speech..."

Does "aleph-bet" sound familiar? It should! While it is the first two letters of the Hebrew lettering system, it's also the foundation for our English word "alphabet"! In fact many English words come from Hebrew...but ours isn't the only language affected by Hebrew in this way.

The Hebrew language, founded upon their lettering system, is one of the oldest known languages...in fact, it might be THE oldest. Most linguists agree that many of the words in our modern-day languages have their roots in Hebrew. For instance, consider that the names of people BEFORE the Tower of Babel incident were distinctly Hebrew. We see this in names like "Methusala" which is a Hebrew word meaning "his death brings" (The flood occurred in the year that he died! Many biblical names hold prophecy like that.) Before the Tower was built, the Bible tells us that all of mankind had one language. From the names before the Tower we can easily see that

29

the first language was Hebrew. But, as fascinating as that is, that isn't WHY we should dive into this language....we should dive in because of its significance to God.

God chose Abraham and his descendants to be his chosen people. He chose Abraham and everything about him – including his spoken language. God ascribed meaning to each of their letters and numbers in a way that no language that I know of does. The Hebrew language is alive and enduring!

Matthew brings this importance to light when he says in Matt 5:18:
     "Surely I say to you till heaven and earth pass away, one jot or one tittle will by no means pass from the law till all is fulfilled."

The Greek word for "jot" is iota. Does that sound familiar? But what's even more fascinating is that the word iota is defined as the Hebrew letter "yod". The Greek word for "tittle" is keraia and it means "the horn of a letter". Greek doesn't have horns on it's letters... they are very curvy. But Hebrew letters have horns! And often times they are important in distinguishing one letter from another. For instance these two examples of the Hebrew letters daleth and reysh:

ד ר

     You can see that the daleth (on the left) has a "horn" that sticks out and that's really the only way to differentiate the daleth from the reysh.

So, what Matthew is saying is that not even the smallest letter or even a tiny PIECE of any other letter will be lost. Why didn't Matthew just say, "not one word"? He was expressing the importance of the Hebrew language itself. It's only now that many Christians around the world are beginning to see its importance in our faith.

Again, I encourage you to become familiar with the letter meanings and number meanings, if you haven't done so, yet. Each letter began as a pictograph and morphed into the modern forms, yet they still hold the same meaning. Something I've noticed, and found most helpful, is that normally two meanings can arrive out of one word using the letters – one meaning in the natural and one in the super-natural. That's not always the case, but it is often.

For example when I looked into the word "fruit" for the phrase "fruit of the spirit", I could see two possible meanings depending on whether the context is talking about fruit in the natural or fruit in the supernatural. Often, but not always, this is a difference between looking at the letter meanings only or looking at both the letter and number meanings.

Fruit - Opari - וּפְרִי
 Vav-pey-reysh-yod
 Natural: Joining together the mouth of man with the work of his hands (he eats what he grows)
 Vav is a nail that also means joining things together. Pey is a mouth. Reysh is a man. Yod is a working hand or a finished work.
 Or...
 Fruit of the spirit – Opari Haruach - וּפְרִי הָרוּחַ
 Vav-pey-reysh-yod | heh-reysh-vav-cheth
 Supernatural: Combining what is most important with speech and deed. This is revealed by He who is on high and bound to the innermost place of man. (It is He who moves the least to become the greatest through the power of El Shaddai.)
 Vav can mean combining. Pey means speech. Reysh can mean what is most important. Yod is a deed. Heh means reveal. Reysh can mean the highest. Vav can mean bound to (nailed to). Cheth means an inner room (often alluding to the inner man). And that last sentence in parentheses comes from the word "Holy" (qodesh – spelled qoph-daleth-shin) to tell us which spirit gives these fruits –

the Spirit of Holiness, or the Holy Spirit. Qoph means least, but its number, 100, means children of promise (a part of the family of God - the greatest that any man can be). Daleth means movement. And Shin means El Shaddai.

So, as you can see, if you're looking into things of eternal importance, using the whole language – letters AND their numbers - makes a big difference!

Pronouncing the letter sounds is quite easy for most letters: the first letter in the written form of the letter is it's sound. For instance, Aleph normally makes a soft "a" sound like "ah" or "aw" but is some-times silent, the beth makes a "b" sound, the gimel makes a hard "g" sound, etc.

Here are the exceptions:

Vaw can make a "v" sound or a hard "o" sound or a "w" sound. (You can see that in the above Hebrew word "opari" – that "o" sound is spelled with a vav.) Cheth may look like it's pronounced "ch" as we would in the word "cheese", but it's actually a guttural mouth sound as if you were pronouncing a hard "kh" sound. Teth can be either a hard "t" sound or a softer "th" sound. Shin can be either an "s" sound or a "sh" sound.

There aren't a lot of vowel sounds in the letters themselves, so you'll often see dots or underlines atop or under letters so that you know the vowel sounds that accompany each consonant letter.

The pronunciation isn't that important as you study on your own, but if you're going to share your awesome Hebrew words with people, you might want to know how to say it correctly!

When you get started with this, make a journal of all the words you study. At first, your word studies might feel clunky and awkward (I know mine did!). You might find yourself in doubt about whether you heard from the Holy Spirit correctly. To that I say two things: First, don't give up. Can you imagine where you'd be if you gave up learning how to ride a bike just because you felt unsure of yourself, awkward, and clumsy? You're going to feel those things but don't think of it as failing- think of it as falling off your bike – just get back up and try again and you'll find yourself at ease with it in no time. And secondly, when you have doubts about how you've interpreted the letters and numbers, look at the word again, pray about it, and examine it through the lens of scripture. Does your interpretation line up with the Word of God? Then that's good enough for now. As long as your word study doesn't do damage to God's reputation with others, you're still on steady footing. You may decide to go back through your notes and adjust some things as you grow in this study habit, or you may go back later to find you've done the word justice! Don't give up, keep pressing on, remain humbly teachable, and you'll do just fine!

With that in mind, I wanted to show you something regarding the Hebrew language that the Holy Spirit showed me. One day while I was worshipping, I looked at the aleph-bet as a whole and it almost looked like it had a natural flow from aleph to tav. So I asked the Holy Spirit to show me if that were so...and He did! Here is what came out of the letters and numbers from beginning to end:

Father, א
Son, ב
and Holy Spirit ג
move ד
to reveal ה
the nail ו
that pierces ז
to separate from ח
the snake ט
in a finished work. י
The palm of his hand כ

33

urges forward ל
his many מ
sons and daughters נ
to support, ס
experience, ע
and command פ
the harvest צ
of the least of these. ק
The insufficiency of man ר
is consumed by His sufficiency ש
in a never-ending covenant. ת

The gospel message is spelled out in the Hebrew aleph-bet! Hopefully you can see how exciting this is! This excitement for this kind of study opened my eyes even more to the wonder and awe of God and his intelligence. I suddenly wanted to hear from Him more and know how to hear from Him better. I found out all I really needed was to know him...but maybe in a way you hadn't considered. What does it mean to "know" Him?

Yada – To Know – יָדַע

Psalm 46:10 -

"Be still and know that I am God; I will be exalted among the nations, I will be exalted in the earth!"

Do you want to truly know the Lord? Be still and yada, or know, Him. Be still. It's so simple, yet in our hurried western lifestyle and Greek mindset, being still is useless – a waste of time. When we think of accomplishing important things, we think of doing and saying. As in - what do I have to do or say in order to be useful? But God's approach – and the Hebrew approach – is to be still. Sure, work needs to be done throughout the week, but in ancient Hebrew culture sitting and learning were just as valuable. We see that played out in the social acceptance of a group of grown men following behind a teacher or rabbi in the New Testament and in Jesus' acceptance and encouragement of Mary sitting at Jesus' feet to learn. We also see that in the way that God begins our day – in Hebrew culture the day has always started at sundown. Which means your day begins when your work is done and it's time to be still and rest. In God's timing our day begins from a place of rest.

You might be thinking "I rest and sit still during my time with

God all the time!". That's a good start but it goes a bit deeper than that physical act.

The word for "be still" there is "rapha" and it a stillness of body, soul, and spirit - a rest for your whole being!

And this is a rest of your body and mind as you "yada" or know the Lord. This word is used both to mean a form of worship AND when a man has sex with his wife. This is a word meaning to "know intimately". So this is a winning combination - rest your body and mind as you seek his face in your mind so that you can spend one-on-one time with him - not to ask a barrage of questions or talk nonstop because that's not rest. No. Rest your mind as you seek simply to see his face and then allow him to fill your mind with images of you and Him doing something together. Just BE with him.

But you might say - well, when do we ask for things in our prayers? Surely there's a time for that! Yes, definitely- throughout the day randomly or after your intimate time with Him. But even in this, you will Let Him Lead by first asking "What would you like me to do for you today?" And you might get an image of a person you should call and pray for or an image of you giving, or praying for a stranger, etc. Even if you get nothing at first, keep trying! And then, yes, it's appropriate for us to ask God for our earthly needs – after our intimate time,...but not before. Let me make my case for why:

Logically speaking, asking for stuff during a time of intimacy is a mood crusher and makes us feel like intimate time is a chore. For instance, if my husband invites me upstairs for some "alone time" and I say "yes", a certain setting and mood is implied, correct? I'll come upstairs to find the lighting has been dimmed, romantic music fills the room, and my husband's full attention is on me - not only with his eyes but also with his words of adoration. But watch how the mood changes if I open my mouth and say "Hi, honey....umm thanks for asking me to come see you...there's a LOT around here that I need your help with, like: the kids, my job, and plus my mom is getting on my nerves so if you could talk to her about that, that'd be great. Also, can you give me some money for tomorrow? Thanks!" And then I either stick around for a few minutes to see if anyone else comes to mind to ask about or, worse, I count that as "alone time" and I leave.

Where's the intimacy in that??!!

But....if I take this intimacy thing seriously, I will set the mood by putting on some love songs (worship music), dimming the lights (closing my eyes), and sitting on the bed/chair to focus all my attention on my Jesus (resting my mind and body to only focus on seeing his face...just to be with him).

After we have enjoyed time together - me just adoring him with my words and my mind focused on seeing him and hearing from him - THEN we can talk shop...things he'll tell me he wants from me and me asking for things I want from him. But all that comes AFTER we've engaged in one of the most meaningful aspects of marriage - intimacy.

In fact, Jesus made this plain when he said in Matt 6:33 "Seek first the kingdom of God and his righteousness and all these things will be added unto you."

"These things" he described earlier were necessities like clothing and food.

The Greek word for "seek" there also means worship or desire. This sentiment is reiterated in Psalm 27:8 -

"When You said, "Seek My face," My heart said to You, "Your face, Lord, I will seek.""

The Hebrew word for "seek" there ALSO means to worship:
Seek - baqash - בָּקַשׁ
beth-qoph-shin
Within the mind of the children of promise is a divinely appointed time to consume the Savior, El Shaddai.

That last letter is either pictured as teeth, heart chambers or fire....it's a letter of passion in consumption - in consuming his presence I am on fire for him!

A time when we "consume" each other or "take each other in" sounds like intimacy and worship to me!

Another word for "kingdom" there is "realm" and the definition of "righteousness" is "freedom from guilt or sin".

So, when we want to meet with him, we start with worship where we are seeking his face in His realm (heavenly places) - a place where we are free from sin and guilt because of the sacrifice of our savior. And when we do that...he has promised to take care of all our needs. Worship first. Ask for needs after. THAT is yada.

There are numerous biblical examples of this kind of waiting on the Lord in order to know the Lord in an intimate moment. One excellent example of this is found in the story of Hanna and Elkhana. I love this story because in her moments in the temple on her face before the Lord she demonstrates 2 kinds of waiting on the Lord: rapha (be still) with yada (intimate worship) PLUS the daily patience of waiting for God to bring the desired blessing and make it manifest. This is so good...

Let's start where the story starts in 1 Samuel 1 – with Elkhana's genealogy:

The root word of Elkhana means "obtained by God". He is the son of Jeroham "compassion", the son of Elihu "He is my God", the son of Tohu "the lowly one", son of Zuph "the overflow of honey".

Reading through his lineage looks very similar to the verse "He seats me (tohu) at his banqueting table (zuph), his banner over me (elihu) is love (jeroham)." And the result of that is one who is obtained by God (Elkhana). And as we'll soon see, his son Samuel means "God heard me". God wooed Samuel's whole family before him in order to bring about one who is heard by God and who hears God....which is exactly what started Samuel's ministry - hearing God call him. Amazing.

Now Elkhana's wife Hannah had no children, but his other wife Peninnah did. And Peninnah continually teased Hannah about it.

Hannah means both "grace" and "mercy".

Peninnah means "jewel".

But all that glitters is not gold. Elkhana valued grace and mercy (Hannah) more than jewels (Peninnah) as scripture points out that he loved Hannah and always gave Hannah a double portion for the yearly temple sacrifice. Scripture does not record him saying he loved Peninnah. Maybe that's why Peninnah teased Hanna constantly. Jealousy can create bullies.

And in 1Sam 1:6 it says that Hannah's rival provoked her. The word there for rival is tsara and the root word, tsar, means "a pebble in a tight place". Peninnah might have been as beautiful as a jewel but even a jewel in the wrong place and time can be a nuisance or aggravation. That jewel was an annoying pebble in Hannah's shoe... probably Elkhana's, as well.

Despite Peninnah's attempt to anger and sadden Hannah, she went to the temple on her own, sat down, and prayed. She started first with reverence to the Lord of Hosts and recognizing herself as his "handmaiden" (servant). Let's look at her whole prayer:

"Then she made a vow and said, "O Lord of hosts, if You will indeed look on the affliction of Your maidservant and remember me, and not forget Your maidservant, but will give Your maidservant a male child, then I will give him to the Lord all the days of his life, and no razor shall come upon his head.""

1 Samuel 1:11

She asked to be "remembered" (we'll see that word again) and not forgotten. Eli, the priest, saw her lips moving and thought she was drunk so he rebuked her. After she explained to Eli that she was not drunk - just praying- Eli blessed her. Before she left, she said "may your handmaiden find favor in your sight". The word there for favor has a root word that means "supplication"...she was asking him to pray for her!

And the word there for handmaiden is different than previous. When she was talking to God she referred to herself as His "ama" - a servant. But speaking to Eli she referred to herself as his "shifkha" - a servant who lives as part of the family. In other words she understood the hierarchy- God is over the whole family of Israel and inside that family, she is a servant. She understood and embraced her humble position in ministry: God-Eli-Elkhana-Hannah.

39

V19 said her husband "knew" her (yada) and God "remembered" her. This isn't like God said "Oh yeah! I had totally forgotten Hannah, but now I remember!" No...the word there actually means "marked". In other words, God marked her for conception. Amazing.

And when Hannah gave birth, she named him Samuel which means "God heard me".

Why did God hear her and remember her? Well, notice the way in which she approached the Lord: she approached him in reverence- not angry at him or accusatory towards him. She didn't blame him for her barrenness and turn to another God, thinking Yehova hadn't blessed her so she'd simply seek another God. No. She approached him in humility as a servant asking her Lord for his mark on her life. And mark her, he did - several times over with many more children. She was "still" in her knowing of the Lord, and she patiently waited day by day for conception and birth.

Like Hannah, we want to birth things in our lives. We get frustrated when it doesn't seem to be happening with us. But the order of things is important: First we understand that we are betrothed to be married, then we make sure to carve out daily intimate times with the Lord, and THEN he makes us "pregnant" with a new spiritual gift, or a new ministry, or a new level of joy, etc. If you want birth, you must first undergo times of intimacy.

Birth from intimacy. Intimacy from marriage....

Dodi - My Love - דּוֹדִי

Song of Songs 6:3

"I am my beloved's, and my beloved is mine. He feeds his flock among the lilies."

If we, the church, are to be the bride of Christ, then accepting our identity as the bride is the first step. You can't get married if you don't accept who you are. That denotes a recognition of our God-given identity. Do you know that in the first tabernacle the laver used for washing after sacrifice was made from the offering of the ladies' brass mirrors? They literally offered their image bearers to the Lord that it might provide a reflection to the priests as they washed. When you wash yourself in the water of the word, are you also offering your identity to the Lord to be changed into his image of you? in order to receive our true identity from our Father we must exchange what we think of ourselves in the way of every aspect of our identity: sexual identity, national identity, job identity, personal identity, etc.. One of those identities is that of the bride.

What characteristics typically represent a bride-to-be?

1. <u>Faithful and devoted.</u> No matter how a bride feels each day she remains faithful to her groom and devoted to his leadership. She knows her groom. She knows who he is and who he isn't so she won't create a false image of who he is. She won't give her love to that false image. We must read scripture, worship, and pray regularly in order to know Him and know how to please Him.

2. <u>Excitement!</u> She is excited over the prospect of being with her first love forever and excited to invite her friends and family. Do you remember your first touch from your savior? Occasionally, just take a moment to close your eyes and remember when your first love removed your burden of sin and death replacing it with joy and excitement. Remember the time and place but also remember what you felt. Let's regain that excitement and invite others into that excitement!

3. <u>Can't wait to talk to her fiancé every day.</u> Do you have a hunger for time with Jesus? As I stated before - if you lose hunger for meat and veggies, just lock away the twinkies you've been stuffing yourself with and you'll find the hunger for good food again! If you find that you're just spending time with God out of obligation because you've lost the hunger, figure out what your "twinkies" are and lock them away for a time. Even if the thing you love to do is a good hobby, if it has taken away your hunger for time with God, then it's a twinkie. Put it away and watch your hunger for God return!

4. <u>Constant preparation in every free moment!</u>

Throughout the gospels, Jesus repeatedly used wedding analogies to portray our relationship and the Kingdom of God. He was speaking to Jewish people, so it makes sense to look at the wedding customs in Israel at that time to fully understand these parables.

So what does preparation look like for a Hebrew couple at that time? Let's first look at how it all begins:

Ancient Hebrew weddings were done in 3 phases: Shiddukin, Erusin, and Nissuin. In the Shiddukin, the first step, the fathers chose their child's mate and made a tentative agreement, or covenant, with the father of the mate they wanted for their child. When the match-up was first agreed upon, there was a dowry involved. The father of the groom had to give a dowry to the father of the bride because the father of the groom would be taking a household helper from her father and adding her to his own home as a helper. In Hebrew this dowry is called a mohar. For us, this match-up happened long ago when God promised the mohar to Abraham (our earthly father of faith) and then gave the promised mohar to the children of Abraham – the mohar was the promised land and a great nation of people. But the people were wayward in their commitment to remain true to God – they "married" themselves to idols and became unfaithful, so God had them exiled from their mohar and gave them the promise of another mohar – the life of the kinsman redeemer, the Messiah. Only a kinsman redeemer could marry a woman in his family who has lost her husband. As a human race we had walked away from our intended husband, shacked up with a new lover who promised us everything and gave us nothing (idols), and then the Father offered up his son as our kinsman redeemer, bringing us into his family once again as his bride.

Once the fathers solidify this covenant agreement, the next step happens when the children come of age - the betrothal (erusin). Unlike our typical engagement period, the erusin was considered marriage in every aspect except for living together. After the erusin, the couple was legally married. The erusin is performed publicly in the town center for all to see. At this ceremony, the families of both bride and groom are present, the ketubah or wedding contract is read and accepted. Gifts are given from the groom to the bride - usually in the form of 10 coins that a woman would wear on a headdress (match this with the parable of the lost coin). The groom pours wine into a cup, then passes it to his bride. If she takes the cup and drinks, she accepts. If she pushes it away, she rejects it. If she accepts, the groom then takes and drinks.

Then the groom says, " You are now consecrated to me by the laws of Moses and I will not drink of this cup again until I drink it anew with you in my father's house."

Sound familiar? It's what Jesus spoke to his disciples at the first communion:

"Jesus took the cup, gave praise to his Father, gave it to them, and said: "Drink from this, all of you". This is my blood of the new covenant which will be poured out for many for the atonement of sins. I say to you, I will not drink from this time forth (from now on) from this fruit of the vine until that day when I drink it new with you in the Kingdom of heaven."

Matthew 26:27-29

The disciples had definitely seen at least a few erusin ceremonies growing up, so they knew this phrase all too well, so when they heard Jesus speak those words they knew the betrothal had begun!

In fact, this betrothal was prophesied long before:

"I will betroth you to me forever; I will betroth you in righteousness and justice, in love and compassion. I will betroth you in faithfulness, and you will acknowledge the Lord."

Hosea 2:19-20 NIV

The word for "acknowledge" is yada – again pointing toward our need for intimacy with Yehova in worship.

The word for "betroth" there is the Hebrew word "aras" which is the root word of "erusin".

Betroth - aras - ארש

 aleph-reysh-shin

 The leader and the person most important to him are consumed with each other.

That's a great picture of what happens when two people have gotten engaged to each other – they are consumed with each other!

The betrothal lasts for about a year, but the groom doesn't know the exact day of the marriage celebration - only the Father of the groom knows. In order to keep themselves holy during the betrothal time, the couple would keep separate from each other and the groom's best friend would relay messages, much like the Holy Spirit does for us during this time that we are waiting for Jesus' return! The bride would also spend more time with her mother learning how best to please her new husband in all areas of life, just as the Holy Spirit teaches us how to please Jesus in all areas of life. Whether we see the Holy Spirit as Jesus' best friend or our mother, the Holy Spirit fits both roles very well!

So, what are the preparations that Jesus is doing now and what preparations should we be doing as we wait?

During the betrothal time, the groom prepares the coming feast and builds an addition onto the house. In Hebrew culture the newly married couple didn't move away from their parents into a new apartment, but rather the groom would build an additional room onto his father's house. When his father says the room is ready, only then can the groom come for his beloved bride.

And that brings us to a very important phrase found in Song of Songs 6:3:

"I am my beloved's and my beloved is mine."

In Hebrew this is: Ani le-dodi ve-dodi li

The Hebrew word for beloved, or "my love" is fascinating:
    Beloved - dodi - יֽדוֹד
    daleth-vav-daleth-yod
    A door nailed to another door by His hand.

Can you see the image God is showing us in this word? This word is what Jesus promised us when he said, "I go to prepare a place for you." His love means he will marry us, provide a place for us in heaven (his father's house) and live with us forever. A beautiful promise spelled out in the letters of one word.

So what does the bride's preparation look like? What are we to do during this betrothal time?

Revelation lets us know that there is definitely preparation to be done by us:

"I saw the Holy City, the new Jerusalem, coming down out of heaven from God, prepared as a bride beautifully dressed for her husband."
    Revelation 21:2

During the betrothal period, as the bride, our preparations are to:

    1. Purchase our adornments and clothing
    2. Keep our wedding garments on at all times
    3. Keep our oil lamps trimmed and lit
    4. Listen for the wedding trumpets.

Let's take each of those one at a time:

Adornments:
    Rev 21 gives us a glimpse into the gems that the bride will wear:

gold, jasper, sapphire, agate, emerald, onyx, ruby, chrysolite, beryl, topaz, turquoise, jacinth, amethyst, pearl.

These gem names have meanings according to their root words:

Shimmering, blood covered, sought after, new life, brightness, written record, overcomer, an instrument in his hand, a flame, a dream realized, courage, purified, polished, and a word of great value.

Recently gem experts have revealed something interesting about these gems. All of the gems the Lord picked for his bride are known as anisotropic gems. This means when we expose these gems to cross-polarized light (pure light), they turn into all the colors of the rainbow. Other gems called isotropic gems (like diamonds and rubies) lose all color and turn black under cross-polarized light. John didn't know this when he wrote the book of Revelation, but God knew!

With these qualities you and I are going to be radiantly beautiful to behold outside and inside!

Clothing:

Rev 19:7-8 tells us what the bride will be wearing and how she attains it:

"Let us be glad and rejoice and give Him glory, for the marriage of the Lamb has come, and His wife has made herself ready. And to her it was granted to be arrayed in fine linen, clean and bright, for the fine linen is the righteous acts of the saints."

Pure linen is the righteousness of the saints. Where does our righteousness come from? His sacrifice. His grace. My salvation. I'll wear it every day. I'll never take it off. Those around me will see it all over me and I'll invite them to come with me.

When the betrothal year is almost at an end, the Hebrew bride and her attendants will begin to wear their clothing and adornments every day – they would even sleep in their wedding clothes! Why? Because they never knew the day or hour that the groom would be coming....in fact, it was often in the middle of the night! Which is why the next item is so important...

Oil:

In the parable of the 10 virgins, some of them run out of oil for their lamps and are left behind when the marriage supper starts. Oil almost always symbolizes the Holy Spirit. He is the fuel for my light. On the wedding day the groom will likely come at night so the bride's light will be the one He's looking for. I cannot borrow oil or let it run out. So I'll keep it filled daily by going to the one who sells the oil - the only payment he asks is my time and attention (being still and knowing Him).

I will trim my wick, because an untrimmed wick produces a lot of smoke but not a lot of light. You may know of people like this – you see the smoke so you assume there must be fire, but the closer you get to them, the more you realize they are all smoke and no flame. This happens when God burns up distasteful, unholy qualities in us but after he's burned it up, we still cling to them because they are familiar and comfortable. But if we want to burn brightly for him, we'll exchange those ashes for beauty (the Hebrew word for "beauty" is "bridal crown"). So we must fill our lamps daily with the oil of his presence and trim our wicks regularly to allow that new oil to burn brightly for that day when he comes to get us for the wedding supper – the nissuin! Which leads us to our final preparation...

Listen:

When the time came for the wedding the groom would lead a procession of relatives and friends through the streets blowing trumpets to announce their coming! Shama, the Hebrew word for hear, actually means "attentive listening and obeying". This isn't a passive hearing. We are to attentively listen for his coming daily.

And so, finally, at the right time the Father will tell his son to come get us for the marriage celebration. In Hebrew wedding tradition once the groom and his procession reach the bride's house, 4 men bring out a bier (a bed with for handles) so that the bride might be carried away from the house...in fact, this tradition of carrying the bride on the wedding bier is called "flying the bride away". Does that sound familiar?

"Then we who are alive and remain [on the earth] will simultaneously be caught up (raptured) together with them [the resurrected ones] in the clouds to meet the Lord in the air, and so we will always be with the Lord!" – 1 Thessalonians 4:17

Then, finally, we will fully be his bride and He will be our groom.

Bride - kalla- כַּלָה

Kaph-lamedh-heh

Covered by redemption obtained through blood sacrifice, she is guided by good teaching and proudly displayed in the grace she is clothed in.

Bridegroom - khathan - חָתָן

Cheth-tav-nun sofit

In a new beginning, protection is provided, a covenant is made and kept, and life is produced. At the right time, he will enact grace producing deliverance, renewal, rest, and jubilee.

While this celebration is one that we can only look forward to in the future, there ARE celebrations we can enjoy with the Lord and his people now. Afterall, another way that God speaks to us is through his Moedim – his appointed times. So, in the following chapters let's talk about New Moon Festivals and the feasts!

The Father's Love Language In:

God's Appointed Times

Moedim - Appointed Times – מוֹעֲדִים

Leviticus 23:4

"'These are the Lord's appointed festivals, the sacred assemblies you are to proclaim at their appointed times:"

Colossians 2:16-17

"So why would you allow anyone to judge you because of what you eat or drink, or insist that you keep the feasts, observe new moon celebrations, or the Sabbath? All of these were but a prophetic shadow and only have symbolic value of what would be fulfilled, for the body is now Christ!"

You may think it strange that I included this verse out of Colossians which seems at odds with the verse in Leviticus and at odds with what I'm about to teach in this chapter. But they are not at odds at all! As I stated before, no one is (or should be) insisting that you MUST celebrate these feasts. I'm only saying that you CAN as part of your adoption, for symbolic value now, and for practice for later (Zech 14:16). In fact, notice that Leviticus tells us these sacred assemblies are to be "proclaimed" at their appointed times. And notice that Colossians 17 puts these feasts in their place – they are a prophetic shadow and evidence of things to come! So, we can proclaim them for what they are – a prophetic picture into what has come to pass and what WILL come to pass. In this way God is speaking to us through His appointed times.

We're going to look into those prophetic meanings, but first let's lay some groundwork.

The first thing we should remember regarding any of God's prescribed feasts – most involve a day (or more) of rest. In fact, the only two instructions regarding Sabbath are to rest and keep it holy, but most other feasts involve rest, as well. So, if you're going to start following the feasts, do it out of rest, not stress.

What does your weekly sabbath or feast sabbaths look like?

Are you at rest? I mean completely at rest - your body AND your mind. I don't mean you can't do anything that requires your brain, but our constant phone scrolling and news watching puts stress on our minds and elevates cortisol so consider cutting down or fasting it completely on your Sabbath day.

Are you keeping it holy? What kinds of shows are you watching or what music are you listening to? Throughout the week each day we fill ourselves with content that, while maybe not evil, is not completely holy, either. Is your sabbath different than the other days - consecrated and set apart- or is it the same?

. . .

I'm going to challenge myself and you to truly follow these sabbath instructions: one day out of the week I'm going to rest my mind and body as much as humanly possible which means putting away social media and news programs. And I'm only going to read/watch/listen to content that I know is holy - sermons, worship music, biblically based books and movies, etc.

If we're really going to take the sabbath seriously I think this is a good challenge for all of us!

The second thing I think is important to remember about feasts is that there are elements that God prescribed for each feast and then there are human additions. You might notice, for instance, there are certain foods, readings, or games that are traditional for each Hebrew feast – yet God never told the people exactly what they must eat or read or play at their feasts. If you would like to add these human traditions to your feast days, that's great! But don't get hung up on feeling like you must do the feast days in exactly the way that modern Hebrew people do. It is enough to celebrate them in the simplicity that God prescribed in His word.

You will also notice that this list of feasts does not include some Jewish holidays such as Channukah or Rosh Hashana – this is deliberate. This list is only a list of biblical feasts prescribed by God. There are many other Jewish holidays that you can celebrate, if you wish, but they are not a part of the moedim – God's appointed times. That's what we'll be focusing on here.

. . .

Finally, remember that Jesus celebrated these feasts while he was here on the earth. The Father instituted these feasts, Jesus celebrates them, and the Holy Spirit always points the way to Jesus. Celebrating these feasts will help us get to know the character of God and his intent in his plan better. And that's always a good thing!

(Side note: I will be mainly pointing out the spiritual significance of each feast with some basics on how Christians can engage in each, but for a more detailed look at how to celebrate these as a Christian I highly recommend a book called "Bring Shalom to Your Home" by Holly Eastburg.)

With all of those principles being understood, let's look at the feasts and what they prophesy:

The Spring Feasts (fulfilled at Jesus' first coming):

Passover	Nisan 14 (April-May)	The Crucifixion of Jesus
Unleavened Bread	Nisan 15-22	Burial of Jesus
Firstfruits	Nisan 17	Resurrection of Jesus
Shavuot	Sivan 7 (May-Jun)	Coming of the Holy Spirit

Monthly

Rosh Chodesh	First of each month	Devotion of Believers

The Fall Feasts (to be fulfilled at Jesus' second coming):

Trumpets	Tishri 1 (Sept-Oct)	Rapture and Resurrection of Believers
Atonement	Tishri 10	Second Coming of Jesus and Judgement
Tabernacles	Tishri 15-22	Marriage Supper

Because these feast days hold such prophetic meaning, let's look deeper into God's instructions for each feast and how they pertain to us as believers.

Rosh Chodesh – New Moon - רֹאשׁ חֹדֶשׁ

Isaiah 66:23

"And it shall come to pass
That from one New Moon to another,
And from one Sabbath to another,
All flesh shall come to worship before Me," says the Lord."

In Isaiah 66 we find God giving an encouraging word to Jerusalem, Israel, and the whole world regarding a peace and prosperity that will return to Israel when the King returns. Verse 23 is one of the more curious bits as it seems to be alluding to the fact that ALL mankind will be worshipping Him on Sabbath and the New Moon celebration. So, if we're all going to be worshipping during the new moon celebration or "head of the month" (Rosh Chodesh) then maybe we should study this celebration!

One of the mentions of Rosh Chodesh shows us that worship with music and a blowing of the trumpet in victory is involved:

. . .

Psalm 81:1-3
"Sing aloud to God our strength.
Make a joyful shout to the God of Jacob.
Raise a song and strike the timbrel,
The pleasant harp with the lute.
Blow the trumpet at the time of the New Moon,
At the full moon, on our solemn feast day."

However, most of the celebration, as outlined in Numbers 28:11-15, involves animal sacrifice...so how do we celebrate it now, as we no longer sacrifice animals? Though Jesus paid the ultimate price, I do believe that God still asks us to sacrifice aspects of our lives to him in trust and faith. So I did a deep dive. I wanted to know God's heart in prescribing these sacrifices. Why those animals? Why those bread ingredients? Why wine?

The Bible gives numerous references to the symbolisms of these animals and bread and wine:

2 YOUNG BULLS -
Significance: great economic sacrifice. Bull or ox represents strength and work. A second reason can be found in the aleph-bet where the pictograph of an ox is the letter Aleph and one of it's meanings is "tame". Strength that is uncontrollable is no good to anyone, but strength that is tamed by the master is extremely helpful! 2 brings us from one new moon to the next.

* * *

1 RAM -

Significance: it is an intact (not castrated) adult sheep. He is an adult - full of strength and "grown-up" freedoms and he has produced children.

7 MALE LAMBS A YEAR OLD -

Significance: meekness, innocence, submissiveness, ability to have children later.

1 lamb for each day of the week. The turning over of our submission should happen daily.

Also: Christ is the lamb of God who takes away the sin of the world.

Each of these animals was to be sacrificed WITH:

Certain amounts of fine flour mixed with oil -

Significance: flour is food. This is an offering of thanksgiving and gratitude. Oil signifies gladness and celebration.

AND...

Certain amounts of wine -

Significance: victory and rest. God only told the Israelites to begin offering drink offerings after they gained complete victory over the promised land...and for every victory after.

PLUS...

1 MALE GOAT AS A SIN OFFERING -

Significance: related to sheep but more aggressive. Almost always used as a "scapegoat" to take away the sins of a people.

. . .

So, what about God's heart can we surmise from his prescribed sacrifices each month? We start with this certainty: God is deliberate. Nothing he does is by accident. That means that he prescribed these specific sacrifices for a reason. He was conveying a message to his people in the sacrifices he required.

Considering that, and combining the symbolisms of each animal and item, our offering each month might be a prayer that sounds something like this:

"Lord, in this new month, take my job, my strengths, the money I earn, my adult freedoms, children that I have, children I may someday have, and my total submission to my Savior, and use them for your purposes.

I give them with gratefulness (flour), knowing that you will always provide. I give them freely and joyfully (oil), knowing that in the midst of the battle I already have the victory (wine) and, knowing all that - I can rest."

Also...

"I give my sins to you in confession - not only so that I don't repeat it like a dog returns to his vomit, but also so that I don't live in condemnation under it. I do this knowing that my sin is wiped clean, so I have the victory."

. . .

After all of that God says something that is repeatedly said after prescribing sacrifices - He says that our sacrifice is a "a fragrance that is sweet unto the Lord."

Or:

Reakh-Nihoah Yehova

That word "sweet" is ONLY used in the Bible to describe His reaction to our sacrifice.

Nihoah – sweet - נִיחֹחַ

nun-yod-cheth-cheth

A life-giving work of the Holy Spirit that results in new birth and eternity.

So when I offer my sacrifice of praise and all aspects of my life to God, I am spraying on myself a perfume called "I'm coming home soon!" And that is God's favorite perfume.

If you want to dive deeper into each monthly Rosh Chodesh, go to blueletterbible.org and do a search for any month like "second month" or "ninth month". There are also numerous teachings on each month online – one of them is my YouTube channel (shameless plug here), titled the same as this book! I think you'll find, as I have, that God has a theme for each month that can be seen in what he has done in scripture during that month. Even the meanings of David's appointed captain each month coincides with God's theme! It really is fascinating!

But, let's not stop with this feast...let's look at the others!

Pesach – Passover - פֶּסַח

Exodus 12:12-14

"But the blood on your doorposts will serve as a sign, marking the houses where you are staying. When I see the blood, I will pass over you. This plague of death will not touch you when I strike the land of Egypt. This is a day to remember. Each year, from generation to generation, you must celebrate it as a special festival to the Lord. This is a law for all time.."

Passover – Pesach – פֶּסַח

Phe-samech-cheth

Letters: At your entrance I will turn aside from your inner room to protect you.

You can even see the shape of the doorway (which was painted in blood) in that last letter!

As Christians, I think we're all familiar with the story in Exodus 12 of the exodus of Moses and the Israelites out of slavery and into freedom through some amazing miracles. This is also where God instituted the month of Passover, Abib (later called Nissan), as the first month of the year. And then God tells them that the 10th-14th days of this month carry some very specific instructions which will lead to their salvation and which will become a Passover celebration for them.

So, what were these instructions?

1. Take one spotless lamb per household or split a lamb for two small households.
2. It must live with that family for 3 days.
3. It must be killed the next day (the 14th day of the month)
4. Its blood must be applied to the top and sides of the doorframe with a hyssop branch.
5. Each family must cook it with fire (not raw or boiled) and it must be cooked whole, from head to legs.
6. Each family must eat ALL of it. Anything that remains is burned in the fire.
7. Each family must be dressed for a quick exit while they eat.
8. This night the Lord will execute judgement against the Egyptians by killing all the firstborn. But he will pass over any house that is covered by the blood.

If we look closer, we can see so many parallels to our final sacrifice of Yeshua on the cross:

Just as the Israelites had been in captivity in Egypt for 430 years, so the people of Israel had been held captive by a cone of silence (no prophecy) for 430 years before Christ's coming. Malachi was the last prophet before Christ and his last prophecy was of a messiah to come.

Just as Passover happened on the 14th day of the first month, so Christ's crucifixion happened in 14th day of the first month.

Just as the lamb needed to be perfect, so Christ was perfect.

Just as the lamb needed to live amongst the people for 3 days and after that they would kill him, so Christ's public ministry was among mankind for 3 years and then they killed Him.

Just as the blood needed to cover them for their salvation, so Christ's blood needs to cover us for our salvation.

Just as the blood was applied on the top and sides of the door and would drip on the ground below, so Christ hung on a cross with the bloodiest parts of him in exactly that same formation.

Just as the blood was applied with a hyssop branch, so Christ was offered vinegar wine on a hyssop branch.

Just as the lamb's body was not to be broken but was to remain whole, Christ's body was not broken.

. . .

Just as the lamb went into the fire, so Jesus went down to the fiery pit of hell after death in order to redeem any there who would follow Him.

Just as the lamb was to be completely consumed, so we are called to consume all of who Christ is (not just the easy parts) - so much so that we begin to become like him.

Just as no foreigner could partake of the Passover meal, but only people who had been circumcised and followed God's law, so too foreigners to Jesus cannot glean the benefit of his sacrifice - only those who choose to follow Jesus and have been adopted into his family can gain eternal life through the lamb's sacrifice.

And after all that just as they needed to be dressed and ready for departure, so we too are now called to be dressed (in our garment of righteousness) and ready for departure for when Christ returns.

In the end, he will judge us as innocent or guilty based on who has Christ's blood applied to them.

So how do we, as Christians, celebrate this feast? As I mentioned before, there are 2 ways we can approach each feast: either in the simplicity of God's original instructions or starting with those instructions and then adding in some of the more modern traditions. The modern traditions are interesting to participate in because not only do they often point out obvious parallels to Jesus, they also allow us to better understand our Hebrew brothers and sisters so that we might introduce Christ to them through these traditions.

If you would like to follow a Christian version of the modern-day iteration of the feast you can create a Seder plate filled with all of the remembrance items and conduct a formal Seder meal using a Christian version of a Haggadah. This is the one we use: go to www.chosenpeople.com and then do a search for "Haggadah".

The day after Passover we roll right into a feast that has always puzzled me, until now – Unleavened Bread.

Hammassot – Unleavened Bread – הַמַצוֹת

Exodus 12:15,17

"For seven days the bread you eat must be made without yeast. On the first day of the festival, remove every trace of yeast from your homes. Anyone who eats bread made with yeast during the seven days of the festival will be cut off from the community of Israel. Celebrate this Festival of Unleavened Bread, for it will remind you that I brought your forces out of the land of Egypt on this very day. This festival will be a permanent law for you; celebrate this day from generation to generation."

Unleavened Bread – Hammassot – הַמַצוֹת
    heh-mem-tsadhe-vav-tav
    Letters: Behold, water and the harvest (grain) are joined together and sealed (in an oven).

.   .   .

The Feast of Unleavened Bread is a week free of leaven - get all leaven out of your house for a week. Anyone who ignores this feast will be cut off from the rest of Israel.

Why is there such a steep consequence for leaven? Let's first look at how the ancient Israelites made both leavened and unleavened bread. Leavened bread was made by separating a small ball of dough from the main ball of dough and setting it aside. While the main part of the dough is put in an oven to bake into bread, the small ball of dough is left out on the counter in order to collect wild yeast spores in the air until it becomes "puffed up". The next time you'd make bread, you would add that small puffed-up ball of dough into your main ball of dough so that the whole loaf will puff up. Unleavened bread is made without that small lump of puffed-up dough.

What does this tell us, spiritually? In Matt 16:6, Jesus tells us to "beware of the leaven of the Pharisees and Sadducees", and as the disciples didn't understand, He further explains.

"Then finally they realized he wasn't talking about yeast found in bread, but the error of the teachings of the Pharisees and the Sadducees." Matthew 16:12

And what was their error? Hypocrisy, self-righteousness, and pride.

When a believer refuses to spend time with the body of Christ, and "forgets" to read the word and worship on a regular basis, his only input is the world. So, he absorbs both the good and the bad in the world – basically whatever is offered to him, he ingests it. Slowly over time, the sin and new ideologies that he has absorbed mixes into his life and leads to pride and he gets puffed up in his pride. And in that pride, he will try to convince other believers that he has found a new way that can be mixed in with the gospel. See...on the outside that ball of yeast dough looks just like the ball of non-yeasted dough – it just looks a little fluffier. Believers may be deceived by this similar looking ball of dough and allow him to mix his puffed-up worldview in with their holy worldview. But, fellow believers, he may look puffed-up and livin large but if you poke holes in his theology with the sword of the Spirit, he'll collapse and you'll see he is only full of hot air! If believers, then, accept this new ideology, they will become puffed up, too – full of hot air - and that whole puffed-up loaf will be placed into the oven.

BUT WAIT! Is there no hope for that ball of yeast before we get to the oven? Yes! There is hope, still! Yeast can be killed in one of two ways - salt or hot water.

Salt: Yeast can be killed by salt but there must be MORE SALT THAN YEAST! Most breads don't contain enough salt - they need to become saltier. In scripture salt is associated with a covenant. The church today needs to be in consistent covenant so that the amount of their salt overwhelms the amount of yeast in the world. So, if that yeast ball wants to kill the yeast inside him, he must pour salt into himself. Christ followers are the salt of the earth, so a yeasty boy can surround himself with salty boys who pour salt into him by speaking the Word of Truth into his life and that salt will penetrate his spirit and soul. Once the yeast is dead, he's now a salty boy, too, and can go bring salt to others!

· · ·

Hot water: there's a reason why God said he'd rather we be cold or hot for him because if you're lukewarm he'll spit you out! Yeast sleeps when cold, dies when hot, but it thrives when it's lukewarm! If your yeast is cold, you aren't puffed up about it - you know it's wrong but you don't know how to fix it so when the promise of salvation comes along you're more apt to take it. So, cold is good. If you're hot for the Lord, the heat of his glory has killed off your yeast which means you are a follower of Christ! Now you just need to stay consistently in his presence to experience that heat daily. But...If you're lukewarm you are proud of your sin and you've elevated your stature to make yourself look awesome in the sight of others. You don't think you need a savior because you've elevated yourself to that position in your life. If, on the day of judgement, your sin (yeast) is thriving then God will spit you out into the oven to be tried by fire.

Now, here's the thing – once bread goes into the oven, the heat kills the yeast bacteria. Scripture tells us that when we enter God's purifying fire, all that is worthless will be burned up and whatever is precious will remain. If you enter into the oven full of yeast – all of those worldly sins and ideologies that you've accumulated along with all of the good deeds you only did for applause – those kinds of things will be consumed by the fire leaving behind empty space where there was once hot air. Instead, during this feast we are asked to physically remove leaven from our homes to remind us of a spiritual principle: the yeast of self-righteousness and pride is worthless in the end and damaging to others along the way.

In developing the Feast of Unleavened Bread long before Christ came to earth, he was drawing a parallel for the Israelites to remember throughout the ages: leaven puffs up just like hypocrisy, self-righteousness, and pride. And self-righteousness is the gateway sin: if I think everything I do is always right based on my own rules for myself, then I can do anything I want! I can perform any sinful behavior and instead of remorse and repentance I will celebrate it and encourage others to celebrate that sin with me. We see that happening all the time now with many social media influencers and this selfie generation. Self-righteousness breeds all kinds of sin - maybe because it was the first sin - from Satan.

In fact, the instruction in Exodus 23:15 says that we should hold the feast of unleavened bread in the week we are brought out of slavery and captivity because "none shall appear before me empty" but the word for empty there can also mean vain. Our pride has to leave so that our innocence and holiness can be given to God as a gift.

But what does unleavened bread have to do with the Exodus?

"So you shall observe the Feast of Unleavened Bread, for on this same day I will have brought your armies out of the land of Egypt. Therefore you shall observe this day throughout your generations as an everlasting ordinance." Exodus 12:17

Remember that God judged Egypt harshly because of their stubborn pride. And leaven is equated to pride. Here God is saying "Get the pride out of you for I am bringing you out of the place of pride." When God brings us out of captivity into freedom, we can't take any of it with us into the next phase. Let it go.

Paul further explains it this way:

"Boasting over your tolerance of sin is inappropriate. Don't you understand that even a small compromise with sin permeates the entire fellowship, just as a little leaven permeates a batch of dough? So remove every trace of your "leaven" of compromise with sin so that you might become new and pure again. For indeed, you are clean because Christ, our Passover Lamb, has been sacrificed for us. So now we can celebrate our continual feast, not with the old "leaven," the yeast of wickedness or bitterness, but we will feast on the freshly baked bread of innocence and holiness." 1 Corinthians 5:6-8

So at the beginning of the year, take this feast week to focus on weeding out any of those attributes in your life and in your home. If you'd like you can also physically get the leaven out of your house as a symbolic act. But even if you don't follow the physical act of getting the leaven out, at least follow the spirit of the feast by asking God to clean the leaven out of your heart. Let's get the leaven of hypocrisy and self-righteousness out of our home this month as we remember his sacrifice to bring us REAL righteousness.

This is also when we begin to count the Omer – the 50 days between Passover and Shavuot, but first we celebrate the Feast of Firstfruits.

Rê'shiyth – Firstfruits - רֵאשִׁית

"The first of the firstfruits of your land you shall bring into the house of the Lord your God. You shall not boil a young goat in its mother's milk."

Exodus 23:19

This Hebrew word comes from "rosh" – the same word and concept as Rosh Chodesh. Re'shiyth means the first in place, time, order, or rank. In the case of this celebration, it means all of those things. We are to bring our first AND our best to the Lord at every harvest time.

Firstfruits - Rê 'shiyth – רֵאשִׁית

reysh-aleph-shin-yod-tav

Letters: The most important and first of what you consume held out in your hand as a sign of your covenant.

. . .

The instructions for Firstfruits were quite simple: Every family that reaps a harvest is to bring a sheaf (a bundle) of the first and best of their barley harvest to the temple so that the priest can wave that sheaf before the Lord. They were also to bring a 1 year old lamb for sacrifice along with flour, oil, and wine. This mandate to give God your first and best was undergirded by the fact that no one could eat any of their harvest until they had submitted their firstfruits offering to God.

We see this concept of Firstfruits coming to fruition in Christ – our firstfruits, for He is the first and the best to rise from the dead into eternity in heaven:

"But now Christ is risen from the dead and has become the **firstfruits** of those who have fallen asleep."
I Corinthians 15:20

Christ was the first to rise from death into eternal life with the Father, making the way for all of us to do the same.

In light of this firstfruits concept, it's important to note a strange phrase that only occurs 3x in scripture, all within sections discussing firstfruits: "do not boil a kid in its mother's milk". Many scholars have been stumped by this phrase because it isn't located in sections regarding food restrictions, only in sections regarding the feast of first-fruits. However, one biblical scholar believes that, rather than this being a literal food restriction, it is more likely that it's an ancient Hebrew idiom.

. . .

Apparently, in ancient Israel some poor farmers, when paying rent or giving their firstfruits offering, would cheat by gathering a lot of last year's stale grain and mixing it with a little bit of this year's new grain and they called it their firstfruits offering. This practice was likely called "boiling a kid in its mother's milk" because of the concept of mixing the old with the new. In this way, they thought they could cheat God.

This concept of giving God your leftovers didn't start with Israel...it started as far back as Cain and Abel. Scripture says that Abel gave a sacrifice of his first and best to God while Cain provided A sacrifice. God did not accept Cain's sacrifice, but he did accept Able's...which led to the first misplaced jealousy which led to the first murder. Cain gave a sacrifice – but it wasn't his first or his best. Clearly, Cain's heart was not in the right place.

While we don't have grain to give as an offering today, I find that many Christians still carry on this practice in their financial offerings and in their time offerings. They count their relationship with God as solid, though they are relying on time they spent with him last month and tithes that they gave last year. This is the same kind of cheating and theft that our Hebrew ancestors engaged in. But God will not be fooled or mocked. Instead, let's treat this feast with the honor it deserves. In everything we give, let us give God our first and our best!

This feast day is a type and shadow of the resurrection of the messiah. Yeshua's death tore the veil, but did you know that at his resurrection the temple doors started opening on their own? Did you know that was a fulfillment of prophecy?

· · ·

According to Hebrew history books (the Talmud) in a section on priestly etiquette and practices we see the nightly routine was to close the temple doors (they were very heavy and took 10 men on each door to close and open), and lock it. Only the eldest priest kept the temple door keys - one key for the outside eastern lock and one key for the northern side lock. Guards were posted at each gate and door. The priests would sleep and then wake before the sun rise. Upon waking they would prepare for the daily duties (assigning duties by lots for cleaning the ash pit, raising the laver from the well, sacrificing the animals, etc). Then they would prepare for the morning sacrificial lamb. When all was prepared by torch light (it's still dark at this point), the temple official would shout "Go and see if it's time for the sacrifice!" A group of men would ascend to the highest part of the temple and watch the east until they could see the sun rising and one would shout "Barkai!" which translates to "Morning Star!". At that moment the priests with the keys would unlock and open the doors. Priestly guards were set in place to assure that only priests could enter.

The Talmud also records that, although this daily process remained the same throughout their history, they record that something strange started happening 40 years before the destruction of the temple in 70 AD and they called it "The Mystery of the Hekel (temple doors)" Here is the mystery....at the 6th hour of the night (midnight), EVERY NIGHT FOR 40 YEARS THE TEMPLE DOORS SEEMED TO OPEN BY THEMSELVES!! This is significant as history also records Jesus' death and resurrection in 30 AD...right at the time that this strange phenomenon started occurring!

Not only did Christ's sacrifice tear the veil signifying open access to the throne of God for any who believe, but upon his resurrection just as he rolled away the stone before sunrise, he also opened the temple doors every day before sunrise! It's as if he was saying "Man will no longer open the doors to only allow access to priests. Look now, my sacrifice will daily open the doors to allow access to all...anytime!"

This was a fulfillment of prophecy!

In Daniel 9, it was prophesied that Messiah will come and then the Temple will be destroyed, but not until He makes open the way.

This was also prophesied in the book of Zechariah:

"Open your doors, oh Lebanon, that a fire may feed on your cedars, Wail, oh cypress, for the cedar has fallen. Because the glorious trees have been destroyed. Wail oh oaks of Bashen, for the impenetrable forest has come down."

Zechariah 11:1

"Open your Doors, oh Lebanon"... the rest of that chapter speaks of the destruction of the land of Israel by the Romans, which occurred in 70 AD, after Messiah came. The Talmud itself says that Zechariah 11:1 prophesied the destruction of the Temple, as the Talmud often refers to the Temple as "Lebanon", since it was made from the trees of Lebanon. They therefore took it to mean, "Open your doors, oh temple, and you will be destroyed." But if the doors are opened on their own then it must also signify that the way to God has been opened!

The rabbis believed that if the doors of the Temple would open by themselves, as by God, this whole prophecy would be fulfilled. This would mean there is a whole new covenant to be fulfilled and that the opening of the Temple Doors in this way would mean Messiah has come.

. . .

Share this story with any Jewish friends you have that it might open up an opportunity to share the gospel with them!

As we finish our study on firstfruits, it's important to mention that we are in the midst of counting the Omer (the 7 weeks/50 days) leading up to the Feast of Weeks. This counting of the Omer holds a lot more significance than I had previously thought.

Chag Shavuot – The Feast of Weeks - חַג שָׁבֻעוֹת

"Then you shall keep the Feast of Weeks to the Lord your God with the tribute of a freewill offering from your hand, which you shall give as the Lord your God blesses you."
Deuteronomy 16:10

Shavuot is celebrated by its 3 names: Feast of Weeks, Feast of the Harvest, and Firstfruits. Harvest is self-explanatory. Though Firstfruits is it's own feast day it is also associated with the Feast of Weeks because while the Feast of Firstfruits is the harvest of barley, the Feast of Weeks, 50 days later, is the wheat harvest. Within this chapter we'll take a look at how both fit into an allegory of God's salvation plan. Now let's take an in-depth look at Shavuot.

Chag Shavuot - The feast of weeks - חַג שָׁבֻעת
cheth-gimel / shin-beth-ayin-tav
Letters: Those set apart are lifted up (Chag), El Shaddai's family

experiences a covenant and a sign that show our deliverance and renewal.

Shavuot means 7 days or 1 week or really 7 of anything. This is from the root word meaning "to 7 oneself" which is to swear an oath because, in ancient Hebrew tradition, an unbreakable oath is created when you declare it 7 times. All uses of the word Shavuot involve an oath or promise.

God showed me something I never noticed before - the purpose behind counting of the Omer between Firstfruits and Shavuot.

There are 50 days between Firstfruits and Shavuot. But they didn't count from number 1 straight through to 50. Instead, according to God's instruction they counted both the weeks AND days, so the counting of the Omer would sound like "This is day 1 which is week 1 day 1 of the Omer...This is day 2 which is week 1 day 2 of the Omer..."and so on. Upon the new week they changed the week's number, but the days started over at 1. For instance, "This is day 8 which is week 2 day 1 of the Omer...".

In modern Hebrew they have distinct names for their numbers, but in ancient Israel, the names of their numbers were the same as its corresponding letter. So, in counting the Omer, they would have said the numbers 1-7 as the letter names aleph-zayin, a total of 7 times each. Remember that when you say something 7 times, you are making an unbreakable vow or promise! According to the meanings of each number (and letter by default) by the 49th day here's what they had vowed:

Aleph x7 - to the Father

Beth x7 - to the Son
Gimel x7 - to the Holy Spirit
Daleth x7 - to the moedim (God's appointed times)
Heh x7 - to the goodness and revelation of God
Vav x7 - to the understanding of my imperfection
Zayin x7 - to the acceptance of God's perfection

In all, here's what their vow would be to God:

I promise myself to the Father, the Son, and the Holy Spirit. I vow to follow His Moedim and behold his goodness and revelations. I vow to understand my imperfection and my need for His perfection.

Furthermore, they were to count 7 weeks but 50 days - that seems like a discrepancy at first, but God is deliberate – nothing is by accident. When you have finished your vows (49 days), you say Aleph one more time - the 8th time - as a way of culminating this celebration by saying:

In these vows I set myself apart for my soon-coming eternity (8) in unity with the Father (1).

Amazing. Mind Blown.

God's instructions for Shavuot were as follows:

1. First harvest your barley just before Passover, then starting on The Feast of Unleavened Bread, count 7 weeks from Passover then harvest your wheat with a sickle and give a freewill offering.

2. Your whole family is to celebrate on this day along with the family of God AND any strangers (gentile believers), widows, and orphans. This celebration is for EVERYONE who follows Yahweh!

3. Remember that you were once a slave in Egypt (God said this often probably to keep them humble that they might more readily obey instruction #2 regarding gentiles.)

Why make these vows in between the barley and wheat harvests? Well, if we think of Passover in light of what it prophesied (Christ's resurrection) and when we think of Shavuot in light of what it prophesied (Pentecost) it becomes evident that the barley harvest represents Jesus and wheat represents us, which we can see in Jesus' parables. So here are some things we know about both:

- Barley is hardy and can withstand virtually any weather or soil condition. Wheat is finicky and high maintenance.
- Barley is more nutrient dense than wheat.
- Barley is considered food for the poor because it is very easy to get and inexpensive. Jesus is "food" for the poor in spirit - the humble who are ready to receive.
- Barley is the first harvest of the year and wheat 50 days later. Jesus was the first harvest: the barley harvest. And at Pentecost the 3000 who were saved were the first wheat harvest.

In addition, we see a foreshadowing of Christ and his church with the story of Ruth and Boaz. Ruth begins harvesting the leftover barley dropped in the field around the time of Passover, just as we picked up bits and pieces of the gospel message before we were saved. Then, by the time the wheat harvest had come along (50 days), Ruth was saved because she was married to Boaz just as we become married to Christ when we accept his salvation.

Incidentally for the Israelites there were a total of 7 main crops harvested each year which in order all coincide with an aspect of our salvation and growth:

"For the Lord God is bringing you into a good land... a land of wheat and barley, of vines and fig trees and pomegranates, a land of olive oil and honey;"
Deuteronomy 8:8

When we consider these crops, we can see them throughout scripture used as metaphors for aspects of our faith:
Barley - hearing the gospel of Christ.
Wheat - becoming a new believer
Grape - wine - victory over death
Fig - Israel - our adoption into the family
Pomegranate – temple decor; abundant life through sanctification
Olives - oil; filled with the Holy Spirit, anointed for assignment
Honey - the promise of a sweet eternal life (honey lasts forever)

For each of these that the Lord blesses us with we are to give a firstfruits offering.

What is our offering today? To receive God's law and its promises the people had to give their allegiance. To receive the promise of the

Holy Spirit the people had to give up their time and attention. And I think those are the 3 things God wants most from each of us - our allegiance, our time, and our attention.

And when our attention is on Him, we'll be ready to hear his trumpet call!

Yom Teruah – The Day of Trumpets - יוֹם תְּרוּעָה

Leviticus 23:24-25

"On the first day of the seventh month you shall observe a day of solemn sabbatical rest, a memorial day announced by the blowing of trumpets, a holy convocation. You shall not do any laborious work [on that day], but you shall present an offering by fire to the Lord.'"

The Day of Trumpets - Yom Teruah – יוֹם תְּרוּעָה

yod-vav-mem / tav-reysh-vav-ayin-heh

Letters: Deeds attached to the flow (of time) to mark the head and to experience the shout of "behold!"

Scripture gives us very little instruction for Yom Teruah except that it is a day of rest, a day for a holy convocation (assembly), and a day for blowing trumpets plus a list of animals to sacrifice: a bull, a ram, 7 lambs, and a goat.

. . .

But the way in which this instruction is given may hold some significance. The phrase used in Leviticus 23:24 is "a remembrance of the blowing of trumpets". If this is to be a remembrance, what are they to remember? The word for "remembrance" is zikarone and its root word zakar means to "mark so as to be recognized". This remembrance is not something that happened in their history that they should remember it, but rather this is a day of trumpets to mark this occasion so that you can recognize it for what it truly is – a call to come home.

And the word for trumpet there, teruah, also holds deeper meaning. Teruah means an ear-splitting sound as an acclamation of joy or a battle-cry - as a shout OR a trumpet blast. Like in Joshua 6 when the walls of Jericho fell. V5 says "And it will come to pass that when they make a long blast with the rams horn and when you hear the sound of the shofar all the people shall **rua** with a great **teruah** and the walls will fall flat and the people will ascend."

Ruah is the root word of teruah and it literally means to destroy. It's figurative meaning is an ear-splitting sound in joy or in alarm. When we celebrate Yom Teruah it is more than just sacrifices, a meal, and some trumpet blasts. Your voice is the trumpet! This is a shout of victory over our enemy as we destroy him with our sound. Yom Teruah is the day of breaking our enemy with sound followed by a shout of joy for we know our day of victory is near! And it will be the same sound we hear when the dead rise and we are called to come home! For us it will be a sound of joy, but for the rest of the world it is meant to be a wake-up alarm!

This feast was created to help us practice for the day when Christ comes to take us home. As such our shouts and trumpet blasts carry supernatural properties. As Christians we can participate in this feast day to help us remember to listen for HIS trumpets which will remind us to be ready and looking forward to that day! The reminder of Yom Teruah helps us reframe our daily lives as we remember that we are not just slogging around with our eyes to the ground, but we have our eyes fixed upon our savior and our ears tuned to the sound of His return. We live our lives in daily anticipation of that day!

As an aside, you may hear this also referred to as Rosh Hashanah, which is not a biblical holiday, but rather a holiday invented to help the Israelites adapt to the Babylonian calendar when they were in Babylonian captivity. And while I'm sure it holds great meaning for the modern-day Israelite, it is not a biblical feast day. God set his calendar so that the beginning of the year was in the month of Nisan/Abib not the month of Tishri. However, to be fair somewhere between the middle of the seventh month and the middle of the eighth month was known as the agricultural new year, so there is precedence for that aspect of the new year. As far as I know there is no biblical mandate to avoid all other holidays, but if the celebrations associated with Rosh Hashanah distract you from the true meaning of Yom Teruah, it's not worth it, in my opinion. Prayerfully seek the Lord on this if you're still undecided on this subject.

Jesus reiterates the importance of practicing this day of trumpets as he gives a list of the some of the terrible things that will happen in the end times:

"Then immediately this is what will take place: 'The sun will be darkened and the moon give no light. The stars will fall from the sky and all the cosmic powers will be shaken.' Then the sign announcing the Son of Man will appear in the sky, and all the nations of the earth will mourn over him. And they will see the Son of Man appearing in the clouds of heaven, revealed with mighty power, great splendor, and glory. And he will send his messengers with the loud blast of the trumpet, and with a great voice they will gather his beloved chosen ones from the four winds, from one end of heaven to the other!"

Matthew 24:29-31

I do find it interesting that this feast is called the DAY of trumpets and not the feast of trumpets. It's almost as if God wanted us to understand that this DAY is important!

In fact, this feast day is known by another name: "the day that no man knows the day or the hour"! Does that sound familiar?

"But of that day and hour no one knows, not even the angels of heaven, but My Father only."

Matthew 24:36

Is it possible that Jesus was using this popular idiom to refer to the Feast of Trumpets being the day of the rapture? This is the only feast day that always falls on the first of a month and is therefore the only feast in which no man knows the day or the hour because no man knows when the new moon will appear until they see it in the sky! This is not definitive, but it seems probable now that we know this feast day's nickname and the event this feast prophesies!

Enjoying this feast as Christians is quite simple, I believe. We can institute a day of rest and gather with our church or a small home group to read scripture pertaining to the blowing of trumpets, share a meal, and then blow the trumpets and shout! We own a small shofar and I highly recommend you get one too or celebrate with a friend who has one. If that's not possible for you, just make a point to give a victory shout to God instead. This feast is a dress rehearsal, of sorts.

So, with either a trumpet blast or a shout let's mark this day so that it will be recognized later!

And after the church is taken up into the clouds to enter into the heavenly realm, there will be many tribulations and then Judgement Day which is prophesied by the Day of Atonement.

Yom Ha'Kipurim – Day of Atonements - יוֹם הַכִּפֻּרִים

Leviticus 23:27-28

"Also the tenth day of this seventh month is the Day of Atonement; it shall be a holy convocation for you, and you shall humble yourselves [by fasting] and present an offering by fire to the Lord. You shall not do any work on this same day, for it is the Day of Atonement, to make atonement on your behalf before the Lord your God."

Day of Atonements - Yom Ha'Kipurim – יוֹם הַכִּפֻּרִים

yod-vav-mem / heh-kaph-phe-reysh-yod-mem

Letters: Deeds attached to the flow (of time) to reveal the Holy Spirit's redemption and renewal for man's inadequate and chaotic words and deeds.

We go from a day of great rejoicing to a day of solemn reflection – the Day of Atonement. You may be wondering why I listed the word as "ha'kipurim" instead of "kipur" and "atonements" plural instead of "atonement" singular. Adding "ha" to the beginning of a word simply

95

means "of" and adding "im" at the end makes it plural. This is the way the Bible lists it, which I think is telling – for many sins there must be many atonements – or one atonement large enough to cover many sins. Thankfully, we have the latter, but when this feast day was created they did not have Jesus, so they needed many atonements to cover their many sins.

Webster's dictionary defines atonement (or expiation) as "the act of making amends or reparation for guilt or wrongdoing", but this complex word requires a more complex definition. The word atonement (kipur) is used just 7 times but its root word (kaphar) is used 103 times as there were many times atonement was required for items, animals, and people. The word kaphar is interesting because its first use in scripture is in Genesis 6:14 when Noah was told to cover his boat with pitch. The word "cover" is used for kaphar instead of "atonement". Further, another related word is used for the actual pitch itself – kopher, which is used literally as pitch/asphalt or figuratively as the price of a life/ransom. All of these meanings are included in the concept of atonement – the act of making amends for sin by covering ourselves with the price of a life. For the Israelites this was achieved temporarily through frequent animal sacrifice, but for us it is achieved permanently through the one-time sacrifice of Yeshua. And just as pitch completely covered the Ark, saving the boat's inhabitants, so Christ's sacrifice is a complete covering of our sins, sealing us for his work.

As such, for us as Christians this is not a time of condemnation, but of conviction. It's a seasonal cleansing of our soul. All year long our being is plagued by this tug of war between the flesh and the spirit as they battle over control of the soul. On this day we call for a cease-fire so that we can assess damage and restate our claim that the spirit should always win. We won't be perfect in it, but each year God perfects us to be closer and closer to it. Before we close this day it's important to throw all of those sins we've reflected on onto our scapegoat. Jesus is our final sacrifice. He ASKS for us to give him our sin so that he can properly dispose of it. If HE forgives you, YOU must also forgive you.

We know that this Day of Atonement alludes to Judgement Day to come, but do we have a full understanding of Judgement Day?

Scripture tells us that we need not fear judgment day, rather it is a day for us to look forward to!

"By living in God , love has been brought to its full expression in us so that we may fearlessly face the day of judgment, because all that Jesus now is, so are we in this world."
    1 John 4:17

Scripture also teaches us something about this day with the term "judgement seat". The word for judgment seat in Greek is "bema" which refers to a reward seat in which we will receive different kinds of rewards according to our actions on earth. We know this is the function of that seat because it is the same word used of the seat a ruler would use when watching the games in a Roman colosseum. At the end of the games, the ruler sitting on the bema would give a thumbs up or thumbs down ruling indicating the winners and losers. The winners were often offered some type of reward.

. . .

"For one day we will all be openly revealed before Christ on his throne so that each of us will be duly recompensed for our actions done in life, whether good or worthless."

2 Corinthians 5:10

What will happen with the good and the worthless? 1 Corinthians 3:10-15 tells us:

"God has given me unique gifts as a skilled master builder who lays a good foundation. Afterward another craftsman comes and builds on it. So, builders beware! Let every builder do his work carefully, according to God's standards. For no one is empowered to lay an alternative foundation other than the good foundation that exists, which is Jesus Christ! The quality of materials used by anyone building on this foundation will soon be made apparent, whether it has been built with gold, silver, and costly stones, or wood, hay, and straw. Their work will soon become evident, for the Day will make it clear, because it will be revealed by blazing fire! And the fire will test and prove the workmanship of each builder. If his work stands the test of fire, he will be rewarded. If his work is consumed by the fire, he will suffer great loss. Yet he himself will barely escape destruction, like one being rescued out of a burning house."

Have you been storing up for yourself treasures in heaven or have you accumulated a bunch of wood, hay, and straw? The good news for us, as believers, is that the bema will be a place of reward, so we can confidently look forward to Judgement Day! In the meantime, we can practice the Day of Atonements each year to reflect on anything the Lord would have us discard or add to the foundation in preparation for the final feast day: The Feast of Tabernacles.

Chag Ha'Sukkot – Feast of Tabernacles - חַג הַסֻּכּות

Leviticus 23:42-43

"You shall dwell in booths for seven days. All who are native Israelites shall dwell in booths, that your generations may know that I made the children of Israel dwell in booths when I brought them out of the land of Egypt: I am the Lord your God.' "

Feast of Tabernacles - Chag Ha'Sukkot – חַג הַסֻּכּות
    cheth-gimel / heh-samech-kaph-vav-tav
    Those set apart are lifted up (Chag) to reveal the support of His covering which is attached to His covenant.

In Lev 23 and Num 29 the Lord calls for the 15th day of the month to be a 7 day feast of tabernacles. For 1 week all of Israel will dwell in tents as a reminder of when their ancestors lived in tents. This practice is bookended by 2 sabbath days and all 7 days are days of sacrifice. Again, though we no longer sacrifice animals, we can sacrifice something...even though for most of us living in a tent for a week IS a sacrifice! Think of it as a newly wed couple giving gifts to each other during their first week together. This feast day is rehearsal for that reality for us at the marriage supper!

Just like the other fall feasts, this is not only a looking back but also a looking forward. Isaiah gives a prophecy regarding the end of days. In chapter 4 after detailing all of the end times destruction he says:

"The Lord will wash away the filth of the women of Zion; he will cleanse the bloodstains from Jerusalem by a spirit of judgment and a spirit of fire. Then the Lord will create over all of Mount Zion and over those who assemble there a cloud of smoke by day and a glow of flaming fire by night; over everything the glory will be a canopy. It will be a shelter and shade from the heat of the day, and a refuge and hiding place from the storm and rain."

Isaiah 4:4-6

And this is prophesied again with more specificity in Zechariah 14 after the war against Israel has been won:

"Then the survivors from all the nations that have attacked Jerusalem will go up year after year to worship the King, the Lord Almighty, and to celebrate the Festival of Tabernacles."

Zechariah 14:16

In the verses following 16, we see that any nation who refuses to attend this festival will experience drought. God seems to place a lot of importance on this feast in His millennial reign.

And we see this concept again in Rev 21:

"And I heard a loud voice from heaven saying, "Behold, the tabernacle of God is with men, and He will dwell with them, and they shall be His people. God Himself will be with them and be their God. And God will wipe away every tear from their eyes; there shall be no more death, nor sorrow, nor crying. There shall be no more pain, for the former things have passed away.""

Revelation 21:3-4

But the good news is we can begin practicing dwelling with him now, not only in the practice of pitching a tent in our backyards for a week, but also by seeking to dwell with him as laid out by Psalm 27.

One morning God woke me at 3 AM with 3 thoughts pertaining to this feast: mindfulness of God's presence as a form of worship, the phrase "I will dwell in the house of the Lord forever", and the word "baqash". I thought baqash may be a Hebrew word...and it was – I found it in the same place where the other 2 phrases are - Psalm 27:4.

"One thing I have asked of the Lord, and that I will seek: That I may dwell in the house of the Lord [in His presence] all the days of my life, To gaze upon the beauty [the delightful loveliness and majestic grandeur] of the Lord And to meditate in His temple."

Psalms 27:4

The word "asked" there means desired, begged, commanded. It's a desperate passionate request- as in "I beg of you - I MUST have it!!" Do we desire his presence like that?

The other action words in this verse are:

Baqash (seek), Yashab (dwell), Khaza (to gaze), Baqar (to meditate). Let's look specifically at the first two:

101

. . .

To seek - Baqash - בָּקַשׁ
    Beth-qoph-shin
    Strong's - to search out either physically or through prayer and worship, to strive after
    Letters: Within the mind of the children of promise is a divinely appointed time to consume the Savior, El Shaddai.

Do we desire to seek him, to crave him, to pursue him, to strive after him, to require him as a necessity? This word is the worship of mindfulness. Throughout the day in the good and the bad are you mindful of him that you choose to seek him?

To dwell - yashab - יָשַׁב
    Yod-shin-beth
    Strong's def: to sit in quiet, to abide, TO MARRY, TO REMAIN
    Letters: To eat with the family

We see this word again here:
    "My beloved is to me the most fragrant apple tree— he stands above the sons of men. Sitting (yashab) under his grace-shadow, I blossom in his shade, enjoying the sweet taste of his pleasant, delicious fruit, resting with delight where his glory never fades."
    Song of Songs 2:3

There's a good reason why Jesus praised Mary for her better choice over Martha's lesser choice. And all she did was sit. Sometimes we complicate things unnecessarily. Jesus doesn't want you to be a super Christian obeying and doing all the right things IF it means you never sit with him. When we sit in quiet with Him, we are choosing to simply enjoy his presence - his grace, the pleasantness of resting in delight of his glory.

Also - this word means to abide. Do you know what abide means? We don't use it often. Abide means a consistent, stable continuing. So to abide in his presence is to stay continually in his presence. You might say - "that's impossible - I need to work and raise kids" and I totally get that - so does God. Instead, see this as continually remembering that he's right there with you and you're right there with him while you work, clean house, wipe butts, etc. I used to set an hourly alarm to remind myself of his presence - the alarm would go off and I'd take a breath, say a quick thank you, and continue on with my day. This mindfulness exercise really did help me to dwell with him more fully. I highly recommend it!

In Psalm 27:4 I think it very intentional that King David wrote kol yomay or "all my days" instead of olam which is "forever". EACH DAY I choose to seek, dwell, gaze and meditate. I will do it with intention and desperation as if I needed his presence like I need the air - because I do.

This entire chapter is regarding a battle David is fighting and in the midst of him asking the Lord to defend him against his enemies he stops at v4 to seek, dwell with, gaze at, and enquire of the Lord. When you're in the midst of trouble is time with the Lord your first move?

And at the end of this song, he ends with a very important word: wait.

. . .

Wait - qava - קָוָה

Qoph-vav-heh

Strong's: bind together, gather together, look, patiently wait

Letters: what is past bound to what will be revealed (as if you asked someone who's waiting what they're doing they might say - "I'm waiting - I've been here for 10 min but something's gonna happen sometime soon!")

It's found in the phrase "Wait on the Lord" or "qava el-Yehova" but is better translated "Expectantly wait as you lean into the Lord". Whether you face troubles or are in relative safety, seek him daily and abide with him hourly so that at any time you need or he needs, you can stop to gaze and meditate while expectantly waiting as you lean into the Lord. This is the worship of mindfulness and the practice of dwelling with Him as practice for our wedding day!

Culmination of the 3 Fall Feasts

We've just finished looking into the 3 fall feasts and the future events they prophecy about.

Now when all 3 of those feasts are done together with the exuberance of his people, let's look what happens:

In 1 Kings 8, (and 2 Chron 5:10) King Solomon has completed temple construction and during the feast of trumpets he brings the Ark of the Covenant along with all other temple items to the Holy of Holies. Scripture says the ark was, then, placed beneath the wings of the cherubim and the wings not only covered the mercy seat but the carrying poles, as well, which extended outside the Holy of Holies! Shortly after placing the ark under these wings, as the people worshipped with singing, cymbals, and trumpets, the glory cloud of the Lord filled the temple!

In 2 Chronicles 7 When King Solomon finished praying over the new temple and the people of Israel, God's fire came down from heaven to consume the sacrifice on the altar and all of Israel fell with their faces down worshipping and saying, "He is good, His love endures forever."

After all 3 of the festivals were over Solomon "sent the people to their homes, joyful and glad in heart for the good things the Lord had done for David and Solomon and for his people Israel."

And we can see all 3 of those feasts in God's response to Solomon:

"If my people, who are CALLED by my name, will HUMBLE themselves and pray and seek my face and TURN from their wicked ways, then I will hear from heaven, and I will FORGIVE their sin and will heal their land... I have chosen and consecrated this temple so that my Name may be there forever. My eyes and my heart will ALWAYS BE THERE"
    2 Chronicles 7:14,16

One day we will be called by his name at the Feast of Trumpets, humbled as we stand before Him on Judgement Day having turned from our sin towards Christ who will pronounce our forgiveness , and then we will dwell forever with He who will always be there.

The Father's Love Language In:

The Night Sky

Mazzaroth vs Zodiac

"He counts the number of the stars;
    He calls them all by their names."
    Psalm 147:4

As you read the title page of this 3rd section you might be thinking "This better not be some twisted attempt to combine New Age philosophy with Christian philosophy!" So let me start by reassuring you – it most certainly is not.

What I AM going to propose is that certain things in God's creation have been stolen from us and twisted by the enemy. See, while the New Age Zodiac is relatively new, the Mazzaroth (the Hebrew people's telling of the story in the stars according to God) is VERY old...about 6000 years old, in fact. Originally, God created constellations for his purpose. And while astrologists use the Zodiac to foretell or prophecy their daily lives, Christians should see the Mazzaroth for what God always intended for it to be – signs that foretell God's plan of love and salvation for his people. Do you see how Satan takes things from us? Do you see how he takes God's message and turns it into a selfish message? He twists God's creation in such a way that we feel like we can't engage with certain animals, things, or people because we don't want to even have the appearance of evil. And while that is a worthwhile goal, we have, by proxy, told Satan that he can have it. Well, I think we're all really fed up with that way of thinking....so let's steal it back! What was once seen as God's messages in the sky, will once again be known as that...so long as we MAKE IT KNOWN!!

Before the 12 major constellations and their 36 decans (accompanying constellations) were known as the Zodiac and its' twisted use of divination, it was known by the ancient Hebrew people as the Mazzaroth and was meant to point to God's plan of salvation for his people.

Mazzaroth is a Hebrew word that only appears in the Bible once in Job:

""Can you bind the cluster of the Pleiades, Or loose the belt of Orion? Can you bring out Mazzaroth in its season? Or can you guide the Great Bear with its cubs?"
Job 38:31-32
The word Mazzaroth means "signs", "constellations" or "garland of crowns" and it comes from the root word nazar which means to hold aloof or set apart as consecrated.

The word "Mazzaloth" comes from the same root word and also means constellations We see it here in 2 Kings 23:5

"He did away with the idolatrous priests appointed by the kings of Judah to burn incense on the high places of the towns of Judah and on those around Jerusalem—those who burned incense to Baal, to the sun and moon, to the Mazzaloth and to all the starry hosts."

Besides this word, there are several places throughout scripture that point to the constellations as being meant for signs in the sky:

"The heavens declare the glory of God;
And the expanse [of heaven] is declaring the work of
    His hands.
Day after day pours forth speech,
And night after night reveals knowledge.
There is no speech, nor language that their voice is not
    heard.
Their voice [in quiet evidence] has gone out through
    all the earth,
Their words to the end of the world."

— Psalm 19:1-4

"Lift up your eyes on high
And see who has created these heavenly bodies,
The One who brings out their host by number,
He calls them all by name;
Because of the greatness of His might and the strength
    of His power,
Not one is missing."

— Isaiah 40:26

"Then God said, "Let there be lights in the firmament
of the heavens to divide the day from the night;
and let them be for signs and seasons, and for days
and years;"

— Genesis 1:14

And then, of course, we have the star of Bethlehem during Jesus birth and again when the Magi arrive to greet the new baby King. In his documentary titled "The Star of Bethlehem" Rick Larson does an excellent job at explaining this star and why the Magi would deem the night sky signs around it so important as to see the need to travel to see this new King.

Clearly God meant for the Mazzaroth to be signs in the sky set apart and consecrated for the purpose of telling his story.

Not only that, but even Matthew ties together the heavens and the letters in this verse:

"For assuredly, I say to you, till heaven and earth pass away, one jot or one tittle will by no means pass from the law till all is fulfilled."

Matt 5:18

Now, having read through the first part of this book you already know that each Hebrew letter has meaning and each letter corresponds to a number which also has meaning.

. . .

Interestingly enough, the word "iota" comes from the Hebrew word "yod" which is the 10th Hebrew letter – it's the smallest letter - and one of the meanings of the number 10 is "the law". A tittle refers to the apex of each Hebrew letter, as every Hebrew letter has a horn-like appendage at the top left. And the Greek word for "law" generally means anything parceled out or distributed (like food for animals) but more specifically it can mean "the law" OR "the gospel". Could it be that Jesus was giving two messages with this one sentence? Could it be that he was not only saying that the book of the law wouldn't lose even one tiny letter or part of a letter until the prophesied end of days, but ALSO that as long as the heavens last – the sky - his letters would last because they display the gospel message in Hebrew in the sky? As I think you'll see both are true as he has not only written his law in a paper book at the hands of men, but he has also written his gospel in the sky with his letters and his salvation story.

I had started reading a book called "Looking Up" by Troy Brewer on God's message in the stars and if you want a more in-depth look at each of these constellations, I highly recommend his book. I mention it, because while the beginning of the book intrigued me, I had not gotten past the first few pages, nor had I seen the constellations yet – just the book intro. In fact, I'd never looked at constellations closely before, having previously seen them as the evil zodiac.

At that time, one morning, in worship, God showed me the stars in the sky. In my vision, he smiled as He looked at me, looked at the sky, clapped his hands then expanded them out revealing all the constellations – not just stars, but the lines drawn between them. Then one Y shaped constellation came out of the sky and flew down towards me but I wasn't scared...in fact, I felt at peace and was in joyful expectation!

. . .

I quickly grabbed my "Looking Up" book and thumbed through the drawn constellations on each page to try to find the one in my vision – it was Taurus...the soon coming judge who will crush our enemy!

Days later I was in worship again, and that same constellation was there in my mind but so was the Hebrew letter Aleph – not as the current version of Hebrew we have today, but the ancient paleo Hebrew version...The original form of the Hebrew letter aleph has the same shape and message of the constellation of Taurus.

The Hebrew letters you see today are the modern renditions. However, by sheer providence we still know what the original Hebrew letters looked like. This image is a comprehensive look at how the letter forms have changed. Please note that though the forms have changed, the meanings have not.

				Ancient Hebrew				Modern Hebrew	
Early	Middle	Late	Name	Picture	Meaning	Sound	Letter	Name	Sound
𐤀	𐤀	א	El	Ox head	Strong, Power, Leader	ah, eh	א	Aleph	silent
𐤁	𐤂	ב	Bet	Tent floor-plan	Family, House, In	b, bh(v)	ב	Beyt	b, bh(v)
✓	𐤂	ג	Gam	Foot	Gather, Walk	g	ג	Gimal	g
◺	△	ד	Dal	Door	Move, Hang, Entrance	d	ד	Dalet	d
𐤄	𐤄	ה	Hey	Man with arms raised	Look, Reveal, Breath	h, ah	ה	Hey	h
Y	𐤅	ו	Waw	Tent peg	Add, Secure, Hook	w, o, u	ו	Vav	v
I	I	ז	Zan	Mattock	Food, Cut, Nourish	z	ז	Zayin	z
𐤇	𐤇	ח	Hhet	Tent wall	Outside, Divide, Half	hh	ח	Chet	hh
⊗	⊗	ט	Tet	Basket	Surround, Contain, Mud	t	ט	Tet	t
⌣	𐤉	˄	Yad	Arm and closed hand	Work, Throw, Worship	y, ee	י	Yud	y
(Ⅲ)	𐤊	כ	Kaph	Open palm	Bend, Open, Allow, Tame	k, kh	כ	Kaph	k, kh
∠	𐤋	ל	Lam	Shepherd Staff	Teach, Yoke, To, Bind	l	ל	Lamed	l
ᴍ	𐤌	𝟸	Mem	Water	Chaos, Mighty, Blood	m	מ	Mem	m
⌐	𐤍	⅃	Nun	Seed	Continue, Heir, Son	n	נ	Nun	n
∓	∓	ᴎ	Sin	Thorn	Grab, Hate, Protect	s	ס	Samech	s
⊙	O	𝑦	Ghah	Eye	Watch, Know, Shade	gh(ng)	ע	Ayin	silent
↶	𐤐	𐤋	Pey	Mouth	Blow, Scatter, Edge	p, ph(f)	פ	Pey	p, ph(f)
⊢	↿	𝓎	Tsad	Man on his side	Wait, Chase, Snare, Hunt	ts	צ	Tsade	ts
Φ	φ	ק	Quph	Sun on the horizon	Condense, Circle, Time	q	ק	Quph	q
Q	𐤒	ר	Resh	Head of a man	First, Top, Beginning	r	ר	Resh	r
ᵜᵜ	w	ﭪ	Shin	Two front teeth	Sharp, Press, Eat, Two	sh	ש	Shin	sh, s
+	×	𝛮	Taw	Crossed sticks	Mark, Sign, Signal, Monument	t	ת	Tav	t

After realizing the similarities between the shapes and meanings of both the letter aleph and the constellation of Taurus, that prompted me to ask – what about the others? And as the Holy Spirit guided me, I found each of the letter matches for each of the 12 major constellations! Once we go through all of these in order you'll see that as we separate each constellation by seasons, 4 words emerge – 12 symbols, each with a story, that also create 4 words painted in the sky so that both the literate AND the illiterate can know God's plan of salvation – God is amazing!

The Constellations

Before we dive into this list, I feel the need to clarify what I meant by placing the constellations "in order". The 12 major constellations travel across the night sky according to seasons. When viewing the night sky from the Northern Hemisphere, you'll notice that certain constellations are visible in certain seasons. There are 3 constellations per season, as seen here:

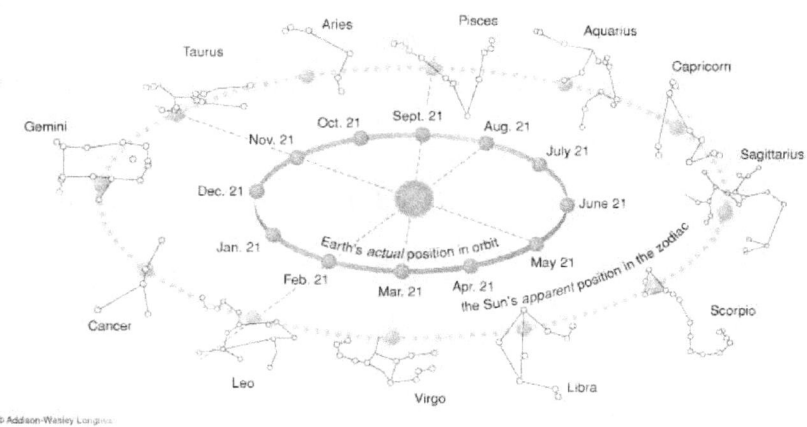

© Addison-Wesley Longman

As you will also see on the following pages, while some of the constellations have lines drawn in the same shape as the letters, some of the currently accepted constellation lines (drawn in black) have had lines redrawn in a thicker grey on top of them to show how the letter adheres to the shape of the placement of the stars, even though it may not match up with the man-made lines connecting the dots.

So, now the question is where do we start? Our Gregorian calendar says that the year starts in January, but that's not what the Hebrew calendar tells us. God told the Israelites that their first month will be the month of Passover – the month of Abib/Nissan. Abib/Nissan starts in mid March, so we're going to start with the first constellation of the Hebrew year: Virgo.

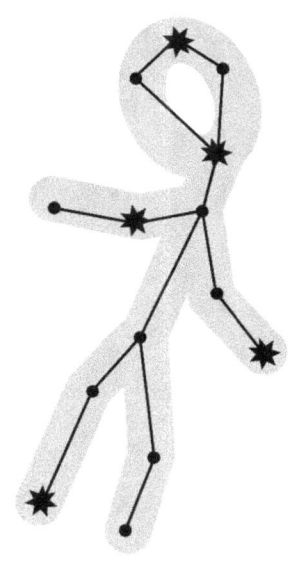

VIRGO = HEH
BEHOLD!

Virgo the Virgin is Heh

"Therefore the Lord Himself will give you a sign: Behold, the virgin shall conceive and bear a Son, and shall call His name Immanuel."
Isaiah 7:14

Meanings of Heh:
Behold, to show, to reveal, revelation, grace, favor not merited, God's goodness, divine strength.

Virgo Star Names:
The branch, who shall come down, the son who comes, he who carries, spike of corn, woman of prophecy, beautiful voice, a long dress, fruit gatherer, gloriously beautiful, God hears.

Biblical Mention:
The star nearest the virgin's head is called "zaniah" in Hebrew and is a shortened form of the biblical name "Azanyah" and it means

"God hears". God hears and begets salvation, as we see in this messianic prophecy through the root word azan, and the word Yeshua:

"Give ear (azan), O Shepherd of Israel, You who lead Joseph like a flock; You who dwell between the cherubim, shine forth! Before Ephraim, Benjamin, and Manasseh, Stir up Your strength, And come and save us (Yeshua)!"
Psalms 80:1-2

The Story:

Because this is our first constellation of the first month rising in the East, it is also the beginning of God's salvation story. Notice that God starts off His starry story with this letter "heh" meaning "behold!". It's a great start to a great story.

This constellation is pictured as a virgin with seed in one hand and a branch from a grown plant in the other. Mary is the only woman to have seed without a man. She holds the seed and will grow it into a man. An interesting correlation between Virgo and the letter Heh is that in Luke's account, the virgin, Mary, is told "Behold" a total of 5 times and 5 is the number for heh. And just as heh means to reveal or to show, God would cause Mary to "show" with pregnancy as he revealed himself through a man born of a virgin.

The enemy's twisted Greek story is that this constellation is a goddess...which is similar to how the Catholic church deifies Mary. However, we know that for her brave role in birthing and raising Jesus she is to be honored but not worshipped.

. . .

In the night sky Virgo is surrounded by 3 companion constellations: Coma, Bootes, and Centaurus. Coma, meaning "the desired son" is a boy sitting on his mother's lap appearing just above Virgo on the side where she holds the branch (as in the branch of David). In 805 AD an Arabian astronomer renamed coma as "ihesu" (Greek for Jesus). Bootes is a herdsman - a shepherd, just as Jesus was and is. And Centaurus is half man half horse which points to Jesus' dual nature as both God and man. Centaurus is the one who pierces Lupus, the victim showing that he will offer himself as sacrifice. All of the companion constellations point to the fact that this virgin who holds seed will bear a son who is the branch of David, the great shepherd, both God and man who will offer himself as sacrifice. Only Jesus fulfills this prophecy in the sky!

LIBRA = TAV
THE CROSS

*These two stars rightfully belong to Scorpio.

Libra the Scales is Tav

"God made you alive together with Christ, having [freely] forgiven us all our sins, having canceled out the certificate of debt consisting of legal demands [which were in force] against us and which were hostile to us. And this certificate He has set aside and completely removed by nailing it to the cross."
    Colossians 2:13b,1∠

Meanings of Tav:
    A mark, a sign, a cross, ownership, to seal, covenant, join two things together, the last, a divinely appointed time to bring deliverance and renewal.

Libra Star Names:
    The cross, the victim, the crown, redemption, weighing scales, propitiation, price and purchase, the price that is deficient and the price that covers (Christ brought these two things together under his covenant)

Biblical Mention:

One of the star names is the Hebrew word "mozanayim" meaning "scales, balances" and appears in this messianic prophecy in Isaiah 40:

"He will feed His flock like a shepherd; He will gather the lambs with His arm, And carry them in His bosom, And gently lead those who are with young. Who has measured the waters in the hollow of His hand, Measured heaven with a span And calculated the dust of the earth in a measure? Weighed the mountains in scales And the hills in a BALANCE (mozanayim)?"
Isaiah 40:11-12

The Story:

What once was a cross in the Mazzaroth was changed by the Greeks to be just another part of Scorpio. Then the Romans changed it into scales to weigh the souls of men by their deeds which is clearly opposite of what God intended. We can see the enemy at work with the change the Greeks made trying to erase Libra by having all of it be included in Scorpio (the enemy). Isn't it just like Satan to try to steal all of the glory away from God and steal any redemption from us? At the foot of this cross are the claws of the scorpion – that's why those stars have names associated with claws because the Scorpio constellation is that close. In fact, two of the stars at the bottom of Libra really should belong to Scorpio as the enemy reaches out towards the cross to attack Jesus.

In the night sky surrounding Libra we have the Crux, Lupus, and the Crown. Crux is a cross. Lupus is often called "the victim" and one of its stars is the Hebrew word "Aseda" which means "to be slain". The crown is self-explanatory. So, in order to accomplish this redemption, the price was paid by the victim on the cross who wears the crown. Yeshua paid this price on the cross to mark us as his own.

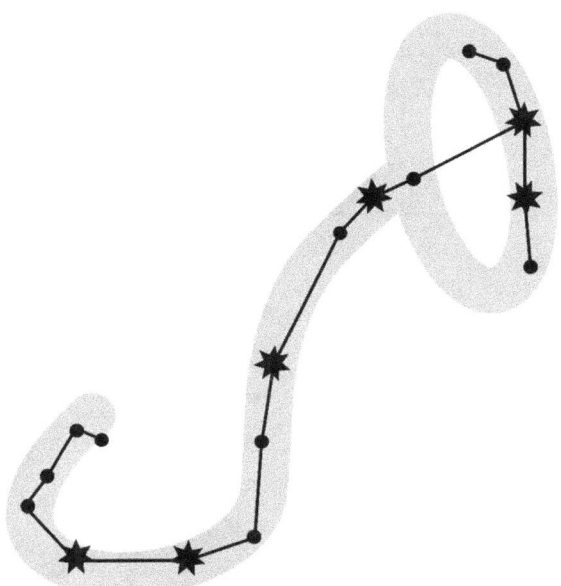

SCORPIO = TSADHE
THE SHARP HOOK

Scorpio the Scorpion is Tsadhe

"And I will put enmity Between you and the woman, and between your seed and her Seed; He shall bruise your head, and you shall WOUND His HEEL.""

Genesis 3:15

Meanings of Tsadhe:

A fishhook, to pull toward, something inescapable, desire, trouble, a harvest, righteous, to hunt, conclusion of a matter followed by judgement.

Scorpio Star Names:

scorpion, wounding him who comes, the wounding sharp tail, fish, a bite or sting, strings of the heart, the destroyer, the perverse, war and peace nebula, Ptolemy cluster (warlike), the three stars at the head were once called "the forbidden tree of life in Eden" (The fruit of which we were forbidden to eat for our protection because we ate from the tree of the knowledge of good and evil.)

Biblical Mention:

Here we see the Greek word for scorpion (skorpios) which is related to the Hebrew word for this constellation: aqrab

"Listen carefully: I have given you authority [that you now possess] to tread on serpents and scorpions (skorpios/aqrab), and [the ability to exercise authority] over all the power of the enemy (Satan); and nothing will [in any way] harm you."

Luke 10:19

The Story:

The Hebrew word for scorpion is "aqrab" which is the name of one of the stars. Aqrab means scorpion but it also means "a knotted whip" and its two root words mean "to wound" and "the heel". Amazing!

The twisted Greek story, however, is that the scorpion killed Orion which is why the scorpion was placed on the other side of the sky to attack Libra, the cross, instead of Orion. Orion is known as the hunter and the light bringer. The bible actually mentions the constellation Orion and refers to it as "kesil" – the fool. Excuse the Star Wars reference, but this paints a picture similar to the Anakin/Darth Vader duality where death (the scorpion) killed and consumed Lucifer, the angel of light. His act of rebellion brought death – not only to all of us through sin, but even death to his previous form as the "angel of light", making him into Satan who attempts to attack Jesus at the cross.

Furthermore, when you look at the placement of Scorpio in the night sky, it is just under the constellation of Ophiuchus who stands on the scorpion while holding a serpent. Ophiuchus is stung in the heel but steps on the serpent's head. Not only that, but another figure, Hercules, is nearby and he is stepping on the head of Draco, the dragon. While Satan's pull, at times, seems inescapable and desirable like the letter tsadhe there is always a fish hook at the end! But as the surrounding constellations show us, Jesus has crushed the head of our enemy. Oh, death where is your sting? It's been crushed under Jesus' feet!

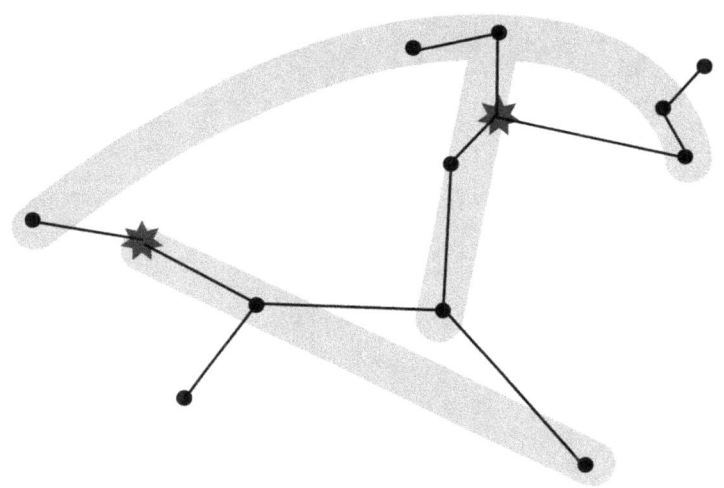

SAGITTARIUS = ZAYIN
THE WEAPON

Sagittarius the Warrior Centaur is Zayin

"Then Jesus made a public spectacle of all the powers and principalities of darkness, stripping away from them every weapon and all their spiritual authority and power to accuse us. And by the power of the cross, Jesus led them around as prisoners in a procession of triumph. He was not their prisoner; they were his!"

Colossians 2:15

Meanings of Zayin:

Plow, weapon, sword, axe, to cut, to pierce, spiritual completion, good, perfect, the inspiration of the Holy Spirit

Sagittarius Star Names:

The archer (kisheth), the beautiful one, musical, the dart, the bow, who comes forth, sent forth swiftly, the riding of the bowman, the prince of the earth, the one who purchases.

Biblical Mention:

In scripture we find the Hebrew word "kisheth" but it is a word that refers to a weapon, not the man holding a weapon:

""The Lord of hosts will visit His flock, The house of Judah, And will make them as His royal horse in the battle. From him comes the cornerstone, From him the tent peg, From him the battle bow (kisheth), From him every ruler together. They shall be like mighty men, Who tread down their enemies In the mire of the streets in the battle. They shall fight because the Lord is with them, And the riders on horses shall be put to shame."

Zechariah 10:3-5

The Story:

Cheiron (Centaur) means "the righteous dealing one" and he was also associated with music and worship (our praise is a weapon!).

The enemy's Greek twist on this constellation makes it appear as if the archer, while trying to shoot the scorpion, is himself wounded by a poisoned arrow and renounces his immortality. The truth is that Satan only WISHES Christ would have denounced his throne in the desert during His 40 day fast, or at the cross. Instead, the mighty weapon DOES shoot and defeat the scorpion.

The decans are the Eagle holding a lyre (stars are: eagle, lyre, music, he shall be exalted), the Altar (stars are: completion, perfection), and the Dragon (punished enemy, head, tread upon). In this constellation we see a perfect picture of Jesus, our Great Defender, cutting down our enemy on our behalf as he goes to the cross to defeat death for us!

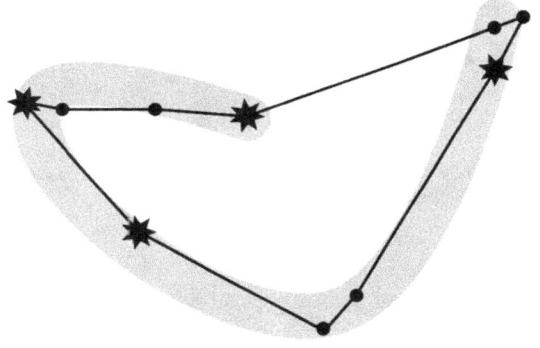

CAPRICORN = LAMEDH
# THE RISEN
# SHEPHERD

Capricorn the Sea Goat is Lamedh

"Therefore, if anyone is in Christ, he is a new creation; old things have passed away; behold, all things have become new."
2 Corinthians 5:17

<u>Meanings of Lamedh</u>:
A staff, rod, to control, prod, urge forward, go forward, teach, learn, tongue, blood of Christ, blood sacrifice, dedication, magnified perfection.

<u>Capricorn Star Names</u>:
Goat, the kid, cut off, the place of sacrifice, the sacrifice comes, the sacrifice slain, the slaying, the record of the cutting off, the Lord (the Judge) comes, the atonement, bowed down.

<u>Biblical Mention</u>:
While "Capricornus" is the Latin name of this constellation, the Hebrew name is "gedi" or "kid" (or young goat). There's a city in Israel named "Engedi" or "fountain of the kid" which we see as an

end-times prophecy of Jesus' reign. In this end-time prophecy the Lord shows Ezekiel a river flowing out of the temple in Jerusalem flowing to the east and west. In the east it will flow into the dead sea and heal its waters so that fish will live in the sea again, which is good news for coastal cities like Engedi AND the fish loosely alludes to Christ followers!

"It shall be that fishermen will stand by it from En Gedi to En Eglaim; they will be places for spreading their nets. Their fish will be of the same kinds as the fish of the Great Sea, exceedingly many."
    Ezekiel 47:10

The Story:

    In light of this scripture in Ezekiel, we see a parallel to this constellation which is typically pictured as a half-goat/half-fish creature. Goats were herded by a shepherd but can also be used to herd sheep and they were used as a sin sacrifice - our scapegoat! A fish is featured in the aleph-bet as the letter nun which also means life. Changing from a goat into a fish is a perfect picture of Christ's resurrection as he goes from being our scapegoat sacrifice to being risen and alive. Just as Christ's death brought him new life, so our death to ourselves makes us into a new creature – we, too, transform from a goat to a fish! His sacrifice and resurrection means our new life!

    The enemy's Babylonian twist is that this is the goat-legged god Pan, who leapt into the Nile River to escape a monster and was transformed. The enemy would have us believe that this constellation representing Christ's selfless sacrifice and resurrection is Christ running away in fear of Satan. Rather this goat represents Jesus choosing to face our enemy head-on to take our sins upon Himself and defeat death by rising from the dead. Our King does not fear our enemy – He easily triumphs over him.

    The surrounding decans are: Sagitta the arrow which has struck Aquila the Eagle who is wounded and falling plus Delphinus which is a fish full of life with its head rising upward. Jesus was our scape-goat, our final blood sacrifice whose death and resurrection made us into new creatures!

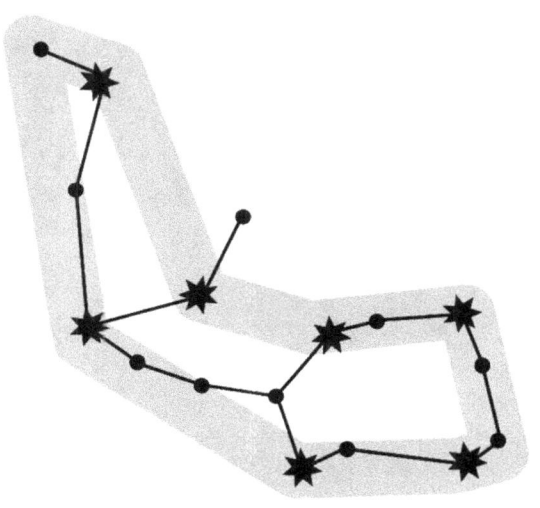

AQUARIUS = GIMEL
THE HOLY
SPIRIT

Aquarius the Water Bearer is Gimel

"It shall come about after this
   That I shall pour out My Spirit on all mankind;
   And your sons and your daughters will prophesy,
   Your old men will dream dreams,
   Your young men will see visions."
   Joel 2:28

<u>Meanings of Gimel</u>:
   Camel's foot, camel rising from its knees, self-will, pride, divine perfection, completeness, lifting up the name of God, Holy Spirit

<u>Aquarius Star Names</u>:
   The happiest of happiness, the water urn, the station of pouring out, the pouring of water, the water bearer, who goes and returns, who causes the abundant overflow, luck of the merchant, luck of the tents, hip bone, the shin, the swallower, the first tent, auspice of auspices (divine or prophetic tokens), auspice of the King, auspice of the tents, three leaders, temple, tomb

<u>Biblical Mention</u>:

One of the Hebrew star names is deli - a water bucket and it's root word dala means water bucket or to lift up (as one does when drawing water up) and is seen here:

"Lord, I will exalt you and lift you high, for you have lifted me up on high (dala)! Over all my boasting, gloating enemies, you made me to triumph."

Psalms 30:1

<u>The Story</u>:

Gimel is a camel rising. Fun fact about camels - they carry water! Not only do they carry water IN their humps but as a pack animal they also carry water in containers ON their humps in order to provide water for their humans. So it's a camel but, being the 3rd letter, it's also the third person of the trinity - the Holy Spirit who has poured himself into us at Pentecost as living water.

The enemy's Greek twist has this image of the Holy Spirit being reduced to a young boy kidnapped by Zeus to become his cupbearer. Satan tries to use this image to diminish the power of the Holy Spirit in our lives. But the joke is on him because we see this water bearer for the powerful Third person of the Godhead that He is.

Its decans also point to this parallel: Pisces Australis (the southern fish) who is pictured drinking the water poured out just as Christ followers drink from the Spirit's outpouring, Pegasus - literally "the horse of the fountain" is a messenger, and Cygnus the swan who was originally known as a dove, just as the Holy Spirit has taken the form of a dove. Throughout scripture the Holy Spirit is attached to the concept of outpouring and the concept of moving water. In this part of the gospel story, the Holy Spirit comes to pour himself into us - living water so that we'll never be thirsty again as seen here:

"Then on the most important day of the feast, the last day, Jesus stood and shouted out to the crowds—"All you thirsty ones, come to me! Come to me and drink! Believe in me so that rivers of living water will burst out from within you, flowing from your innermost being, just like the Scripture says!" Jesus was prophesying about the Holy Spirit that believers were being prepared to receive. But the Holy Spirit had not yet been poured out upon them, because Jesus had not yet been unveiled in his full splendor." - John 7:37-39

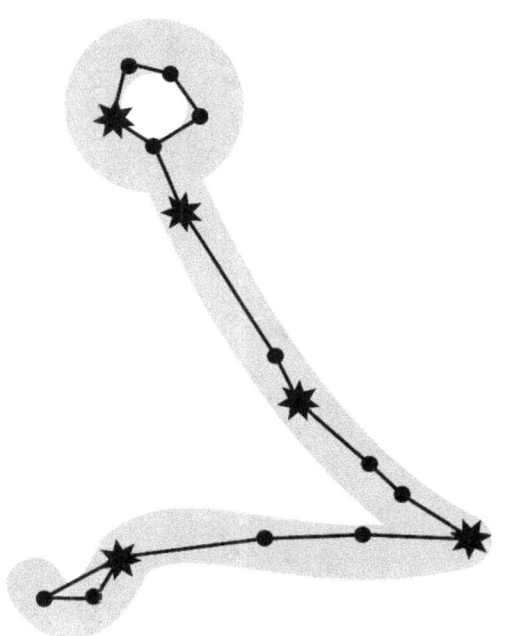

PISCES = NUN
THE FISH

Pisces the Fish is Nun

"Again, heaven's kingdom realm is like a fisherman who casts his large net into the lake, catching an assortment of fish. 48When the net was filled, the fishermen hauled it up on the shore, and they all sat down to sort out their catch. They collected the good in baskets and threw the bad away."
Matthew 13:47,48

Meanings of Nun:

A fish, a seed, to sprout, to spread, offspring, descendant, action, life, heir to the throne, faithfulness, work of the holy spirit, deliverance followed by rest, jubilee.

Pisces Star Names:

The fish, the fish continue, multitudes, the fish of him who is coming, the chord of the fish, mouth of the fish, the cord, rich or blessed, thread or tether, the united, the upheld.

Biblical Mention:

The Hebrew name for this constellation is "Dagim" coming from the root word "daga" meaning fish or multitudes which we see here when Abraham blessed his grandsons:

"The Angel who has redeemed me from all harm— may he bless these boys. May they preserve my name and the names of Abraham and Isaac. And may their descendants multiply greatly (daga) throughout the earth."

Genesis 48:16

And we see the letter nun reiterating this concept in this prophetic picture of Christ:

"May the king's name endure forever; may it continue (nun) as long as the sun shines. May all nations be blessed through him and bring him praise."

Psalms 72:17

The Story:

We start by seeing Aries' (the lamb's) front leg grasping this cord of fish. The lamb has gone fishing! And he has caught two fish swimming in different directions - one is heading north but the other follows the path of the sun. This is a picture of the Israelites and Christians. We are tied together and held by Yah but only one fish is following the Son.

The enemy's Greek version pictures this image as two sex gods escaping a monster by becoming fish to swim away. Only Satan would throw sex in the midst of this to distract us from the deeper sense of camaraderie that we will one day have with our messianic Jewish brothers and sisters.

Companion constellations (decans) include Cepheus (the branch, the redeemer) and Andromeda (the chained woman, the bound, the weak, the afflicted, delivered from hell, set free from death). As the lamb catches the fish and holds the cord to pull all towards himself for judgement day, we will be sifted into two groups - those who swam away from him and those who swam TO him.

152

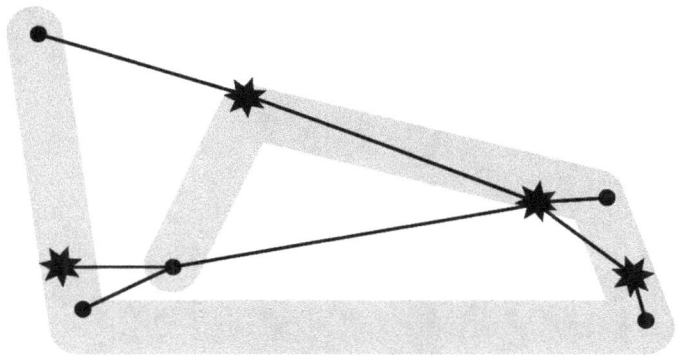

ARIES = BETH
THE VICTORIUS LAMB

Aries the Lamb/Ram is Beth

"Then I saw a young Lamb standing before the throne, encircled by the four living creatures and the twenty-four elders. He appeared to have been slaughtered but was now alive! He had seven horns and seven eyes, which are the seven Spirits of God sent out to the ends of the earth."
    Revelation 5:6

Meanings of Beth:
    Tent or house, the body, the household or family, inside, within, amid, Living Word, God the son, second person of the Godhead, come alongside to hinder or help, difference between good and evil

Aries Star Names:
    The sheep, the lamb, gentle and merciful; the three stars in the head are named "the head", "sign two", and "minister" (Jesus is the head of the church, the 2nd person of the Trinity, and our high priest), finding treasure, a home for captives, reconciliation with a

prince, a king crowned, the bearer, the northern lily, the sacrifice of righteousness.

Biblical Mention:

The Hebrew name for this constellation is Telah (the lamb) and we find it's Greek counterpart here:

"Saying with a loud voice, 'Worthy is the lamb who was slain to receive power, and riches, and wisdom, and strength, and honor, and glory, and blessing."

Revelation 5:12

The Story:

Jesus is the lamb of God who takes away the sin of the world, but in the book of Revelation we see a ruling and reigning lamb who was wounded but is now risen and worthy to open the scroll. It is He who is now adding onto his Father's house to make a home for us. This Aries figure is also holding the bands binding the two fish of Pisces - the fish that represent Israel and gentile believers.

The enemy's Greek version shows this as a ram that a king sent to save his children from an evil stepmother but when the ram returned with the children the king sacrificed this ram, took its golden fleece, and gave it to a dragon to guard. Satan would have us believe that our King was unjust in sacrificing the lamb, and that the dragon (Satan) now holds the power of redemption. We know, however, that the true message of this constellation is that both the Father and the Son (and the Holy Spirit) were in agreement on this plan of salvation which he knew would require a brutal sacrifice, but the benefit of being able to hold his fish (followers) and bring them with him was worth it!

The decans coincide with God's intended story of Aries: Cassiopeia, the enthroned woman, represents the bride of Christ which is visible in the meanings of her star names (the freed, the branch, the enthroned, the seated) and she is seen holding a branch in one hand as she prepares her adornments with her other hand and the king to her right is offering her the scepter. Aries sits atop Cetus, the leviathan (serpent) as the victor. Perseus also appears just as the victorious lamb and according to his star names he is the breaker who steps on the head of the enemy, as he carries the enemy's prisoners (us) away.

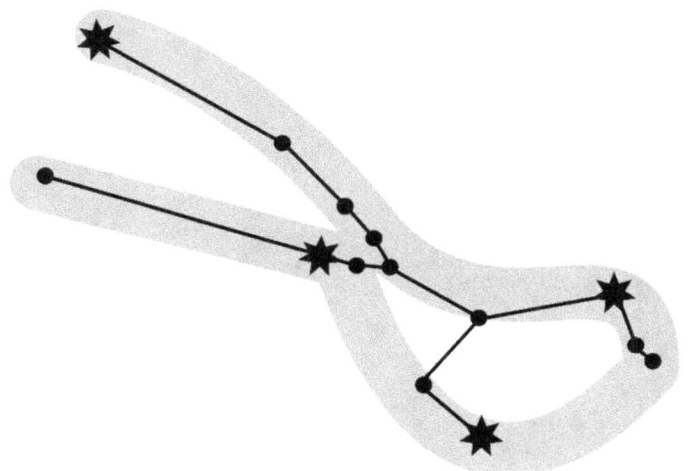

TAURUS = ALEPH
# THE JUDGE

Taurus the Bull is Aleph

"We give You thanks, O Lord God Almighty,
   The One who is and who was and who is to come,
   Because You have taken Your great power and reigned.
   The nations were angry, and Your wrath has come,
   And the time of the dead, that they should be judged,
   And that You should reward Your servants the prophets and the
saints,
   And those who fear Your name, small and great,
   And should destroy those who destroy the earth."
   Revelation 11:17,18

<u>Meanings of Aleph</u>:
   Bull, ox, gentle, strength, Adonai, leader, what is first, the Father,
unity, sufficiency

<u>Taurus Star Names</u>:
   Bull, coming and ruling, leader or governor, the congregation of
the judge, harem of the king, daughters of the king, the center or

foundation, belonging to the judge, the abundance, follow the leader, mighty to save, the mighty chieftain comes.

Biblical Mention:

The Hebrew name for this constellation is "shur" which means "bull or ox" but its root word means coming and ruling. We see this word in Numbers 23 when God spoke to Balaam, and he prophesied:

"God brings them out of Egypt; He has strength like a wild ox (shur)."

Numbers 23:22

The Story:

The enemy's Greek twist behind Taurus is that Zeus made himself into a bull to impress a girl. That is a cheapening of the true meaning behind Taurus. Instead, we see Jesus, as a bull, running towards Gemini (the immortal one giving eternal life to his mortal brother) to take them away with him for judgement day. As he runs, he kicks the sea monster, Cetus, in the head, then passes Orion, the hunter who "comes forth as light" (in Hebrew he is "kesil", the fool which is a picture of Lucifer, the foolish angel of light who became Satan) who is standing on the river constellation, Eridanus, which means "river of judgement". On his way, he also pierces the foot of Auriga, the shepherd who is holding a goat (as the shepherd is allowing himself to be pierced as a sacrifice for sin).

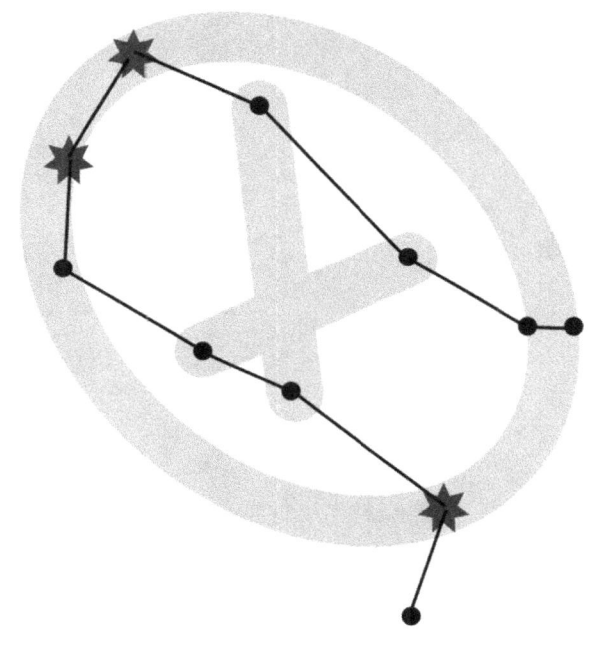

GEMINI = TET
THE ADVOCATE
PROVIDER

Gemini the Twins is Tet

"Soon I will leave this world and they will see me no longer, but you will see me, because I will live again, and you will come alive too. So when that day comes, you will know that I am living in the Father and that you are one with me, for I will be living in you."

John 14:19,20

Meanings of Tet:

Dual meaning: either a snake in a basket or fruit in a basket, provision, good or evil, to surround, to twist, judgement of man.

Gemini Star Names:

The place of him who comes, the branch spreading (making a basket), the palm branch, outstretched (a choice offered), very sweet, to excel, God's ring (as tet is), treading under feet (as He does the snake).

Biblical Mention:

The Hebrew word for this constellation is Teomim which means twin and its root word "ta'am" means completeness by a joining. We see this concept here:

"But the one who joins himself to the Lord is mingled into one spirit with him."

1 Corinthians 6:17

The Story:

The enemy's Greek twist pictures Castor, (on the right) who is holding a weapon (signifying war or a hunt), while Pollux (on the left) is holding the palm branch (signifying peace and victory). Castor is a mortal born of man. Pollux is the immortal son of Zeus. Pollux loves Castor so much that when Castor dies, Pollux asks his father, Zeus, to impart immortality to Castor so that they can live forever in the heavens together. Sound familiar? It's a similar story, but Satan (aka Zeus) has tried to give himself all the glory and praise for this deed – a complete fabrication since he never intended to give us life of any kind, let alone eternal life.

Jesus loves us so much that he will stand in the gap for anyone who believes in Him, knows Him, and follows Him. He desires to be one with us.

Gemini is surrounded by its 3 companion constellations: The hare (Hebrew name: the enemy), Sirius (the prince), and Procyon (the redeemer).

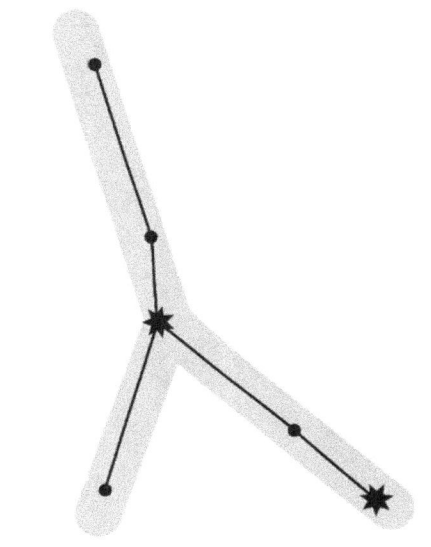

CANCER = YOD
THE GRASPING
HAND

Cancer the Crab is Yod

"Then we who are alive and remain [on the earth] will simultaneously be caught up (raptured) together with them [the resurrected ones] in the clouds to meet the Lord in the air, and so we will always be with the Lord!"

1 Thessalonians 4:17

Meanings of Yod:

A hand closed or closing upon, to work, a deed done, a finished work, perfection of divine order, divinely ordered events, completeness of order, the law.

Cancer Star Names:

He who holds and binds, encircling the possession, embraced, holding, the hiding place, offspring, innumerable seed, assembled thousands, place of good rest, grasping, northern donkey, southern donkey colt.

Biblical Mention:

Sartan (meaning "to hold") is the Hebrew name of this constellation. Its cousin is the word "masoret" which we see here:

""I will cause you to pass under the rod [as the shepherd does with his sheep when he counts them, and I will count you as Mine and constrain you] and bring you into the bond (masoret) of the covenant."

Ezekiel 20:37

The Story:

The original shape was seen as a tightly grasping fist or claw, not a crab. The letter yod is a tightly grasping fist. Much like the image of Aries the lamb grasping the bindings of Pisces the two fish, so Cancer is similar in that the crab's pincers tightly grasp the "innumerable, assembled thousands". The difference is that in Pisces one fish is going its own way while the other fish follows the Son. This time all Christ followers – jews and gentiles - are bound together in the brightest star which is in the crab's torso and it means "innumerable seed" but in modern times it is known as the beehive cluster because it's actually a cluster of innumerable stars! And just like Pisces this cluster constellation contains two classes of these offspring, a northern donkey and a southern donkey as they straddle the innumerable seed. This is a perfect picture of how God has bound both Israeli believers and Gentile believers together and holds us tightly to himself unto eternity.

The 3 decans of cancer also speak to these two groups combining: Ursa Minor (the small bear) has a star that means "the chosen of the flock" just as Israel is, and Ursa Major has stars that mean "wealth of the multitude" and "purchased ones" just as the gentile believers are, and both go into the 3rd decan - Argo, the ship that returns the redeemed to their heavenly home.

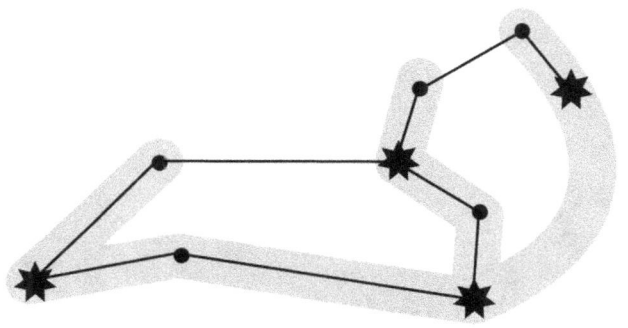

LEO = SHIN
EL SHADDAI
(DESTROYER OF
THE ENEMY)

Leo the Lion is Shin

"Then one of the [twenty-four] elders said to me, "Stop weeping! Look closely, the Lion of the tribe of Judah, the Root of David, has overcome and conquered! He can open the scroll and [break] its seven seals.""

Revelation 5:5

<u>Meanings of Shin</u>:

Teeth, ivory, point of a rock, a peak, flames, to devour, consume, destroy, something sharp, El Shaddai, supernatural victory over enemies.

<u>Leo Star Names</u>:

The lion who rends (lays waste), coming vehemently as a flame, treading under foot, shining or sparkling, the judge comes and seizes, wrapping together, the exaltation, the one who punishes, the enemy thrust down, the judge who comes and seizes violently.

<u>Biblical Mention</u>:

In Hebrew this constellation is called ari "the lion". We find this in a prophecy regarding Judah and the messiah that will come through his line:

"Judah, my son, is a young lion (ari) that has finished eating its prey. Like a lion he crouches and lies down; like a lioness—who dares to rouse him? The scepter will not depart from Judah, nor the ruler's staff from his descendants, until the coming of the one to whom it belongs, (Shiloh - the messiah) the one whom all nations will honor."
Genesis 49:9-10

The Story:
Jesus is the Lion of Judah who will come to destroy the enemy of our souls at the end of days.

The enemy's Greek twist is that this Lion came to earth savagely attacking people and livestock and then Hercules killed him. Satan wants us to be afraid of the Lion of Judah, when we have nothing to fear, for the Lion is our protector! And the enemy only WISHES he could use man to destroy God. In reality the only one who needs to fear the Lion is Satan and his followers, for the Lion is coming to earth to put an end to Satan's plans and set all things right.

The decans of Leo are Hydra (the serpent), Crater (the cup), and Corvus (the crow or raven). Leo is stepping on Hydra's head just like Jesus will crush Satan's head in the end. Crater is the cup of wrath that Leo will pour out upon the earth. And Corvus is the predatory bird that will pick at the carcasses after Armageddon. Jesus will come back as the lamb for those who love and follow him, but he will be a Lion, the destroyer, for his enemy and his followers. Jesus come soon!

The Story From Beginning to End

Having seen all of these constellations in order, I'm sure you can see the big picture from the Virgin Mary all the way through to the conquering king at the end. From the first month to the last, every year God is displaying his plan for us in the night sky, in order so that we might see each event in its proper time.

Virgo, the virgin Mary, carries seed that will grow into a man – the savior of the world. At Libra, the cross, our savior was crucified to satisfy the scales of justice and bring us redemption. Scorpio, Satan, is at the foot of the cross to "bruise his heel" but Jesus has the victory as he aims his weapon, Sagittarius, at Scorpio to "crush his head". In Capricorn, the sacrifice who brings new life, Jesus rises from the dead to bring us victory over death and make us into new creatures. In Aquarius, the Holy Spirit is poured into us like living water. In Pisces, the fish, God's people are given a choice to go their own way or follow the Son! Aries is the reigning and ruling lamb who goes to prepare a home for us and is worthy to open the scroll as he hangs onto his people. Taurus, the Father, will come to judge all on Judgement Day. In Gemini, Jesus has gathered us to himself like a harvest in a basket and will speak to the Father on our behalf, granting us eternal life. In Cancer He holds onto us tightly bringing us home, as Leo, the Lion of Judah, comes to defeat Satan in one final battle to set all things right.

But more than that, I hope you see that we've just created a really long Hebrew word full of 12 letters as they correspond to the monthly constellations. God painted these as images to be understood either in story form for the illiterate or in letters for those of us who CAN read!

Constellations and their corresponding letters in order of appearance:
    Virgo - heh
    Libra - tav
    Scorpio - tsadhe
    Sagittarius - zayin
    Capricorn - lamedh
    Aquarius - gimel
    Pisces - nun
    Aries - beth
    Taurus - aleph
    Gemini – tet
    Cancer - yod
    Leo - shin

This list makes this really long word: התצזלגנבאטיש
    But...is it just one word?
    God asked us to use the Mazzaroth as signs AND seasons. We have 4 seasons, so if we split this list of 12 up into 4 words, while still keeping the same order, we get these words:

The source – התצ

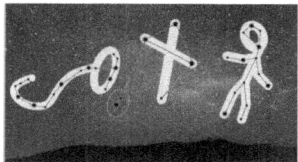

Flowed/Spilled out – זלג

Prophesied/Prophet – נבא

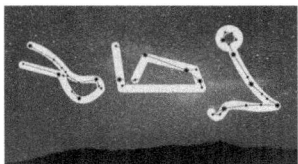

Wedding table – טיש

When we put all four of those words together, we have:

The Source spilled himself out (into man) to prophesy of the coming wedding supper (table). Amazing!

Not only that, but all 3 constellations for each season correlate to the Hebrew word for that season:

The source - Virgo, the virgin, is the source of the newborn messiah; Libra, the cross, is the source of our new life; and Scorpio, the sharp hook, is the source of all evil.

Spilled out - Sagittarius, the armed warrior, spills the enemy's blood; Capricorn, the sacrificial goat, spills his own blood; and Aquarius, the Holy Spirit, spills out himself upon all mankind.

Prophesy/Prophet (also meaning "authorized spokesman") - In Pisces, the Christ followers, are called his ambassadors and prophets; Aries, the reigning lamb, is the fulfillment of prophecy; and Taurus, the judge, is the originator of prophecy.

Wedding table – In Gemini, both the sinner and the sinless, are now bride and groom; Cancer, the hand that holds tight, is the groom's hand holding tightly to mine as he brings me home; and Leo, El Shaddai, will prepare a table before me as he crushes my enemy.

He has made his salvation plan obvious and available to all, just as Romans 1:20 tells us:

"For since the creation of the world His invisible attributes are clearly seen, being understood by the things that are made, even His eternal power and Godhead, so that they are without excuse."

The End and The Beginning –
Achăriyth Reshith - אַחֲרִית רֵאשִׁית

"Declaring the end from the beginning,
    And from ancient times things which have not been done,
    Saying, 'My purpose will be established,
    And I will accomplish all My good pleasure';"
    Isaiah 46:10

"Since we are approaching the end of all things, be intentional, purposeful, and self-controlled so that you can be given to prayer."
    1 Peter 4:7

I'd like to applaud you for getting to the last chapter of this book. You and I have done a lot of mental work as we seek to understand the Father's Love Language more fully. And though you've come to the end of the book, this is hopefully the beginning of a new chapter for you in your walk with Christ. We are also very close to the end of this world and the beginning of a new life, dwelling with our Savior, King, and Groom.

Throughout this book I hope you've seen our Father's intense desire to communicate with us through his language, his customs, and his feasts. I hope that you will begin (or continue) to embrace all aspects of your adoption and begin (or continue) to seek intimate times with Jesus regularly. He SO desires to meet with you each day!

Reader, I may not know you in this lifetime, but if you are listening for His trumpet call, have your wedding garment on, and have your lamps filled I am greatly looking forward to meeting you and getting to know you as we dwell with the Lord forever. I'll see you soon!

Resources

Name	Pictograph	Meaning	Name	Pictograph	Meaning
Aleph		Ox / strength / leader	Lamed		Staff / goad / control / "toward"
Bet		House / "In"	Mem		Water / chaos
Gimmel		Foot / camel /pride	Nun		Seed / fish / activity / life
Dalet		Tent door / pathway	Samekh		Hand on staff / support / prop
Hey		Lo! Behold! "The"	Ayin		Eye / to see / experience
Vav		Nail /peg /add / "And"	Pey		Mouth /word / speak
Zayin		Plow / weapon /cut off	Tsade		Man on side / desire / need
Chet		Tent wall /fence / separation	Qof		Sun on horizon / behind
Tet		Basket /snake / surround	Resh		Head / person / first
Yod		Arm and hand /work /deed	Shin		Eat / consume / destroy
Kaf		Palm of hand / to open	Tav		Mark /sign / covenant

Heh = 5 "h"	Daleth = 4 "d"	Gimel = 3 "g"	Beth = 2 "b"	Aleph = 1 short "a" (or silent)
Behold, to show, to reveal	A door, a path, a way of life, movement (into or out of)	A camel, something lifted up (like a camel rising from its knees), self-will, pride	Tent or house, the body, the household or family, inside, within, amid	Ox, bull, gentle, tame, the leader, strength, what is first, Adonai, thousand, teach
Yod = 10 "y"	**Teth = 9** "t"	**Cheth = 8** "ch" or "kh"	**Zayin = 7** "z"	**Vav = 6** "v" or "w"
A hand (closed or closing upon), to work, a deed done, a finished work	A snake, a basket of food, to surround, to twist, a twisting or coiling	A fence, inner room or chamber, to separate, to cut off from, to protect	A sword, an axe, a weapon, a plow, to cut, to pierce	A nail, a peg, a hook, joining together, making secure, becoming bound (nailed) to
Samekh = 60 "c" or "s" sharp	**Nun = 50** "n"	**Mem = 40** "m"	**Lamedh = 30** "l"	**Kaph = 20** "k"
A prop, to support, aid, assist, a slow twisting or turning aside (like a propped up plant)	A fish, to sprout, to spread, offspring, descendant, action, life, heir to the throne, faithfulness	Water, mighty, massive, many, chaos (like the deep), to come from (like water down a stream)	A staff, shepherd, cattle goad, rod, to control, prod, urge forward, go toward or forward, teach, learn, tongue	A palm of a hand, a wing, to allow, to cover, the power to suppress or lift up
Reysh = 200 "r"	**Qoph = 100** "q" or "k"	**Tsadhe = 90** "ts" or "s" sharp	**Phe = 80** "p" or "f"	**Ayin = 70** " " (guttural)
A head, a person, what is the highest, most important, chief	The back of the head, what is behind, last, final, the least	A fish hook, to pull toward, something inescapable, desire, trouble, a harvest, righteous, to hunt	A mouth, opening or entrance, to command, speak, open, a beginning, here, present	A mouth, opening or entrance, to command, speak, open, a beginning, here, present
Nun Sophith	Kaph Sophith	Phe Sophith	Tsadhe Sophith	MemSophith	**Tav = 400** "th" or "t"	**Shin = 300** "s" or "sh"
					A mark, sign, "x" or cross, ownership, to seal; covenant, join two things together, the last	Teeth, ivory, point of a rock, a peak, to devour, consume, destroy, something sharp, El Shaddai

Modern Hebrew (Post-Babylonian Exile) as it appears today. The ancient meanings remain.

We can easily see the importance Yehova places on these letters as He frequently inserts or deletes a letter from names in order to change the meaning of a name. We see this in the change from Abram to Abraham and Sarai to Sarah. By adding the "heh" God bestowed grace upon them both: Abraham received grace as a forerunner to redemption through his line and Sarai, being a masculine name, was changed into a feminine name with ending "heh" making a barren woman into a mother. Another example is Saul to Paul wherein God took away the destruction of "shin" and added to him the mouthpiece of "phe". God's chosen language is amazing!

1	Deity, unity, sufficiency, the first, God the Father
2	Living Word, God the Son, to come alongside to hinder or to help, difference or division between good and evil
3	Divine perfection, completeness, lifting up the name of God, the Holy Spirit
4	Creation, the world, the material world, the moedim (God's appointed times)
5	Grace, favor not merited, God's goodness, divine strength
6	Enmity with God, weakness of man, falling short, imperfection, number of Man, sorrow, secular completeness
7	Spiritual completion, completion, good, perfect, God's perfection, the inspiration of the Holy Spirit
8	Eternity, new creation, new birth, new beginning, first in a new series
9	Judgement of man, wrath, conclusion of a matter, summation of man's works, harvest, fruit of the Spirit, fruitfulness, duality of good and evil
10	Ordinal perfection, perfection of divine order, divinely ordered events, completeness of order, the law
20	Redemption, doubling of ordinal perfection, expectancy, maturity, accountablity

30	Blood of Christ, blood sacrifice, dedication, magnified perfection of
40	Trials, testing, probation, chastisement but not judgement, grace multiplied by renewal, a probationary period that results in renewal
50	Work of the Holy Spirit, deliverance followed by rest, grace multiplied, jubilee
60	Pride, support, lifted up
70	Perfect spiritual order, punishment and restoration of Israel
80	Magnified ordinal perfection resulting in eternality, new beginning and new birth
90	Conclusion of a matter followed by judgement, combination of ordinal perfection and judgement at the conclusion of a series
100	Children of the promise, God's election of grace, promise
200	Insufficiency of man, inadequate, lacking what is necessary or required, inability to accomplish a required purpose, deficient, the complete sufficiency of God, the adequacy of the eternal, the ransom that is both efficient and sufficient to reclaim what was lost
300	The final blood sacrifice made by the perfect Lamb of God, a divinely appointed time connected to the children of promise, election, supernatural victory over enemies including evil and death; the number connected to the death, burial, and resurrection of Messiah
400	A divinely appointed time that will bring about deliverance and renewal, a period of probation to accomplish a divine purpose

The Ketubah of the Lamb and His Bride, The Church

On the day, week, and year that was seventy sevens, or 490 years, since the command to restore and build Jerusalem, Messiah, the Prince, appeared in the city of Jerusalem. Yeshua, son of Adonai of the triune Elohim said to this maiden daughter of the human family "Consecrate yourselves, and be holy, for I will betroth you to me forever. Yes, I will betroth you to Me in righteousness and justice, in lovingkindness and mercy; I will betroth you to Me in faithfulness, and you shall know Me. For your Maker is your husband, the LORD of hosts is his name; and the Holy One of Israel is your Redeemer, the God of the whole earth He is called. You truly love me, so I will passionately love you and reveal myself to you. You truly follow me, so my Father and I will honor you. My Father and I care deeply about even the smallest detail of your life. Fear not, for I am with you; be not dismayed, for I am your God; I will strengthen you, I will protect you, I will support you with my righteous right hand. Therefore, do not worry, saying, 'What will I eat?' or 'What will I drink?' or 'What will I wear?' For after all these things the others seek. For your heavenly Father knows that you need all these things. But seek first the kingdom of God and His righteousness, and all these things shall be provided for you. According to the law of Moses I present you with the mohar, a marriage gift. Yet this mohar is valued far above the traditional 200 silver zuzim. My father has given me authority over all the human family so that by my sacrifice I may give the gift of eternal life to the bride he has chosen for me – you, the believing church. Dwell with me and I will dwell with you and you will bear fruit."

And, The Church, this maiden, consented with these words "O Yehova, I give my life to you. I will greatly rejoice in you as a bride who continues her preparations. I choose to detach myself from this world and abandon myself to you so that I will find true life and enjoy it forever!"
The nedunya, the dowry, that that the maiden brings from her home is her old sin-nature. And this Yeshua, the said groom, accepted this dowry, adding on His own mattan - the gift, of the Advocate, the Spirit of Truth, making the total an incalculable sum.

And thus said Yeshua, the said groom: "I have taken upon myself the surety of this ketubah, of the dowry, and of the additional sum. I have taken upon myself all of your griefs and carried your sorrows and pains. I was pierced for your rebellion, and crushed for your sin. The punishment required for your well-being fell on me and by my stripes you are healed and made whole so that when the time for nissuin, the wedding supper, has arrived, I will look to you and say 'You have a special place in my Father's heart. Come and experience the full inheritance of the kingdom realm that has been destined for you from before the foundation of the world!'"

And the surety for all the obligations of this ketubah, dowry and the additional sum has been assumed by Yeshua, the said groom. His steadfast love never ceases; his mercies never come to an end; they are new every morning; great is his faithfulness.
Yeshua the groom has said to the maiden "I have established an everlasting covenant with you and I will remember My covenant with you for all your days."
Ve'kanina אקנינא and Telesteo Τετέλεσται: It is finished and paid for.

Witnesses:
"I, John, am the disciple who is bearing witness about these things, and who has written these things, and my testimony is true."

"I, Peter, and the other apostles were eyewitnesses…that, in Jerusalem, he was crucified on a cross, but God raised him from the dead three days later…so that everyone who believes in him receives complete forgiveness of sins through the power of his name."

About the Author

Angie Sickler is an avid student of scripture with a focus on the Hebrew language and culture. She has had the privilege of serving at her home church in various teams and levels of leadership. Angie has also been a guest speaker at numerous churches and conferences such as James Nesbit's Tribe Quantum and The Gateway Prayer Garden in Colorado Springs. She is a traveling speaker and regularly teaches Biblical Hebrew concepts for her followers on YouTube at youtube.com/@TheFathersLoveLanguage-fll and on her FB ministry page at https://www.facebook.com/Sicklers

Angie lives in Northeast Colorado with her husband, daughter, and 2 dogs.

3 TREES
PUBLISHING

A Publishing Assist Company

Honor & Excellence as the Seedbed of Your Written Work

3 Trees Publishing was born the result of an architectural buildout of Wells of SouthGate. 3 Trees Publishing serves to reconnect creatives with their kingdom calling by supplying a framework of excellence for all printed work.

Let the expression of your purpose be revealed as you prepare your legacy in print.

For more information, contact 3Treespublishing@gmail.com

The Destiny Series Books

STRATEGIC TRAINING TO DISCOVER YOU

The Destiny Series is designed to help you discover the who and the why that you are. You are designed to become a great leader that God intended you to be, and you can reach your maximum potential in the ministry that the Lord Jesus gave every person (Matthew 28:19).

This dynamic and interactive series is available for individual or group study, as well as an author led course. To learn more, use QR code to view books now available by Author, Rebecca D. Bennett and much more.

His sound reverberates. Can you hear Him speak your name?

The Name Speaks by author Angela Broussard is an introduction to the Master Poet and His creation: *you.* Engage in the formation of your identity within the context of the Kingdom of God. Come into the knowledge of your vital role of service to the King, displayed within your given name.

* * *

Meet the Architect of Oikos: the Creator-King who fashioned seven pillars of wisdom to sustain Kingdom culture: marriage, family, maturing sons & daughters, stewardship, kingdom economy and creative commerce, authority, and worship. Against the backdrop of Matthew 19, Jesus' encounter with the rich young ruler provides an examination point of current cultural practices. The text exposes the pillars of Kingdom culture in such a way that the reader is able to inspect their arena of influence

for structural breach. *Will you embrace cultural stability to promote growth and maturity? Will you be counted as a reformer?*

The Architect of Oikos & the Blueprints of Kingdom Culture is the second installment of the Doors Gates & Thresholds Series by author Angela Broussard.

God is calling, will you answer?

A Royal Disgrace: I Fell - Now What? Author Dwayne Jacobs exhorts every person plagued by the past: you can find restoration as a son in the Kingdom of God! The gifts and callings of God are without repentance. He does not withdraw what He has given, nor does He change His mind about those to whom He sent His call. This book is about the love of God that draws men to repentance, that times of refreshing may come.

* * *

Prophetic Expressions of His Love: 31 Days of Devotion Face to Face with the Spirit of God is a personal invitation from the Heavenly Father calling you to the secret place, to an encounter in His presence, where discovery of a love beyond comprehension begins as you are tuned to the sound of His heartbeat. Here you come to know Him and are known by Him; Beloved, it's time for you to know who you

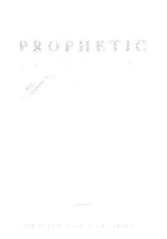

are and what your true purpose is. Each day is a new way to see what the Father sees and to believe what He says. Dare to believe Him with all of your heart and you will see miracles happen all around you. Author Paula Jacobs

As a follower of Christ, you want your life to reflect His love and grace, but your emotions do not cooperate. With thought-provoking questions to help you get to the heart of your issues and the space provided to process your thoughts, *A Christian Woman's Guide to Overcoming Messy Emotions* is a valuable tool. Give yourself (or someone you care about) the gift of biblical truth that equips you to overcome! Author Georgia Pointer

* * *

Big God, Getting To Know Him: A New Believer's Guide To God by Donna L. Bass How big is God? He is BIG! Yet, He is not hidden, or hard to get to know. His ways are available to understand and experience. This set of self-guided lessons are your introduction to God in a BIG way! Inside are foundational truths that will help you journey into an ever increasing relationship with a BIG God. Be a learner and follower of God's ways and discover how BIG His purpose is for you!

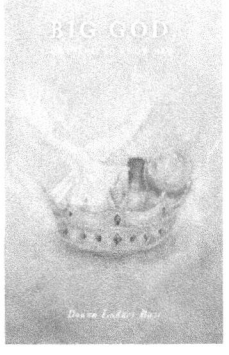

Upcoming Titles 2024:

> *The Barley Company* by Angela Broussard
> *You Can Live Again* by Karla Tyrpak
> *Think On These Things* by Georgia Pointer

Education

MAKING EXCELLENCE VISIBLE

Kingdom Leadership Institute Gulf Coast

KLI GULF COAST

The leadership institute of choice prepares you for leadership in the Kingdom of God. The strategy of Kingdom Leadership Institute Gulf Coast is individualized. Your leadership training can begin at any level of spiritual and ministry maturity. We start where you are with what you do.

As one can function in any aspect of culture, once taught to function in kingdom culture, the Institute educates and prepares students for any arena of occupation. We honor kingdom leaders from every walk of life. Students come from many professions and occupations.

Partnered with KLI Jacksonville, our course intensives develop mature individuals to impact the current culture with Kingdom culture. Determine today to engage your life's work at the starting gate of Kingdom Leadership Institute Gulf Coast. For more information or to enroll, please use QR code or contact us via email at kligulfcoast@gmail.com.

Wells
of SouthGate

Serve, Train, Empower

We Bring the Trainer to You.

- Community Advancement
- Business Training
- Leadership Development

Wells of SouthGate is a training, equipping, and activating center on the Mississippi Gulf Coast.

Our passion is to see each person matured to fulfill our God-given dreams and destiny, to become a flourishing, contributing member of their society. For more information, use QR code to visit the Wells of SouthGate website.